One for the Road

An Anthology of Road Trip Writing

Edited by Proal Heartwell

ISBN 9798653727238

ROAD TRIPS

Introduction 5

One Fine Day Steve McNerney 7

Hot Pockets at the Apocalypse CJ Green 13

Edsel Bahlmann Abbot 17

Distance Learning John Watterson 22

Junior Brown's Porch Francis Wood 25

On Down the Line Dave Krovetz 31

Snapshots from a West Coast Road Trip Bill Dunnington 33

Utah Zack Verham 37

Road Trip John Schoonover 40

Road Weary Tony Zentgraf 42

A Few Cups of Coffee Paul Erb 45

Meditation at Lagunitas Brewery Andrew Deloss Eaton 51

Miles and Miles Corky Schoonover 53

Quarters Chris Poe 57

Trip to Maine Brian McMillen 62

5/3/03 Jay Varney 65

Spring Break Baseball Pilgrimage Sam Carr 71

Goin' to Carolina Michael Kuchinski 75

Two Journeys Home Robbie Sapunarich 79

Travelogue Kathy Zentgraf 85

"Where Have You Gone, Joe DiMaggio?" Jim Barns 87

Never Get Back Cortlandt Schoonover 88

Blues, Bluegrass, and Barbecue Proal Heartwell 94

Spotify Playlist *103*

INTRODUCTION

IN 2015, A GROUP OF FRIENDS AND ACQUAINTANCES, largely in Charlottesville, Virginia, came together to write stories about haircuts, barbers, and barber shops. The resulting anthology, *A Little Off the Top*, was sold online and all proceeds from these sales were donated to the Boys and Girls Club of Central Virginia.

Fast forward five years. When the Covid-19 pandemic sent much of the world into social isolation, it seemed a good time to take on another group writing project, an opportunity to connect with relatives, friends, and friends of friends. And since most of us were stuck at home, why not write about that great American pastime, the road trip? Hence, *One for the Road: An Anthology of Road Trip Writing* was conceived. You will find twenty-three pieces within these pages, and the authors of the offerings range in age from twenty-six to eighty years old. Many of these authors are returning writers who contributed to *A Little Off the Top* five years ago, and the pieces here feature tales of cross-country trips, day trips, and even trips of the imagination. In addition to essays, original poetry and song lyrics are included in the collection.

Speaking of songs, you will find a link to a Spotify Playlist at the back of the book, as well as a roster of the tunes on that playlist. All of the authors were invited to contribute to this list, and many of the songs included are referenced in the respective stories. Others reflect the theme or mood of the piece, or, perhaps, recall a specific time or moment of the author's life. We hope you enjoy this eclectic collection which roughly follows the book's sequence of stories.

Writing these original pieces was a rewarding experience for all involved (or so they tell me), and all proceeds from the sales of *One for the Road* will be donated to local food relief efforts. Finally, it is our hope that this anthology will inspire you to hit the road when circumstances permit. In the meantime, stay safe and stay well.

—Proal Heartwell

ONE FINE DAY

by Steve McNerney

"The real voyage of discovery consists, not in seeking new landscapes, but in having new eyes."
—Marcel Proust, 1923

The story that follows traverses some of my earliest memories. I soak in these remembrances often. Sometimes they are triggered, sometimes they are a result of an intentional journey. These recollections pave a road. A road that transports me back in time. To a time of discovery and wonder. A time of innocence knocking on the revelatory door of life's purpose.

I FRAME MY EARLIEST CHILDHOOD MEMORIES WITH THE streets of Brooklyn. It was here at the age of seven in 1959 that I pledged allegiance to the New York Yankees. And it was here in 1965 that I had my first kiss in the cellar of my Fourth Avenue apartment building. What a thrill it was then when my buddy agreed to take a trip with me back to my old neighborhood.

We exited the R at 69th Street and Fourth Ave. We made our way over to 72nd and found ourselves in front of my old apartment building. At my friend's behest I reminisced aloud about this four-story fortress and surrounding cement paradise.

It was the playing field where I learned to throw, catch, and hit a ball. The arena for flipping cards and tossing pennies. The track for running when I broke a window with a ball. The workshop where I built scooters with my friends. The blackboard for creating a skully board with chalk. The real estate for my initial foray into business with lemonade stands. One block alone had every store I would ever need to purchase sustenance and entertainment should the Russians or Cubans invade. As I stood in the courtyard, flashbacks ensued:

"I got it, I got it! I finally got a Mickey Mantle card."

"Did you see American Bandstand *yesterday? Chubby Checker was giving twist lessons."*

"OK, the fire hydrant is first base."

"That's a do-over. Let's do it over."

"Stephen, go upstairs and tell your mother Marilyn Monroe died."

"Dad, I finally threw the ball up on the roof."

The streets were my classroom away from school. It was in the courtyard of the building issues of grave importance were unveiled and discussed. Mantle or Maris in '61? Why can't I get my hair to look like Ricky Nelson's? Is there a dance called "The Locomotion" or is it just a song? What is the best way to eat a Devil Dog? Who is having sex and what exactly does that mean?

"Hey Ray, Ritchie just told me you gotta put your thing inside the girl." This didn't make much sense to me. "Exactly where am I supposed to put it?"

My mother was not happy when she walked into my bedroom. "What's that smell? What did you put in your hair?" I told her I was trying to get my hair to look like Ricky's. I didn't realize Vicks VapoRub wasn't the same thing as Vaseline.

We walked over a block to the church and school on 73rd. Few institutions have left more of an impression on than the Roman Catholic Church and School I attended. The impact was more than existential as the knuckles on a nun's hand were feared more than the drunk who lived on the first floor of our building or the rats that seemed to purposely hover near our bikes in the cellar. An iron fist indeed! The influence of Catholicism was so strong I viewed my Protestant cousins as something less than whole.

There was a sense of confusion when I walked past one of the Protestant churches. "Is Jesus in there too?"

"Dad, why don't the Protestants have to keep their church clothes on all day Sunday?"

I remember a store on Fifth Avenue that had all of its windows painted black. There was no seeing inside. I was convinced that the store was ... wait for it ... Purgatory. To this day, I can still recite, word for word, my default confession to the priest:

"Bless me Father for I have sinned, it has been a month since my last confession. I accuse myself of being mean to my parents and having dirty thoughts." I am not sure I was really ever mean to my parents, but it seemed wise to throw something else out to take the focus away from those dirty thoughts.

When we revisit something from our childhood, usually we are struck by how small something is compared to how we remember it. This was not the case as we stood in front of the church. It was as august that day as it was fifty years ago. We entered and were both transported back to our Catholic youth by the aroma of incense. Muscle memory led us to the holy water. We dipped our fingers and blessed ourselves.

We were in the midst of another early morning game of slap ball. We played each morning on Play Street before the school bell rang. In the midst of our game we noticed an exodus had ensued. All the kids were running into the church. Not to miss out, we stopped our game and followed suit. One of the younger students had run out of the church to announce the statue of the Virgin Mary had moved. We all remained in the church, hoping to see Mary move (or wink) until we heard the bell ring. Mary did not oblige. The next day life was back to normal and the games continued. I do recall though sneaking peeks at the statue for many Sunday masses thereafter.

We walked down the block to Third Avenue. Passing the school yard on the way, we stopped and talked about the turf wars in the school yard and the pecking order that determined who got to play where.

"We need to go over there to play. Every time we start here the eighth graders just make us move. Last time they even took the ball. Come on, let's move."

I pointed out a specific basketball goal. I vividly recalled shooting baskets there, humming "Walk Like a Man" by the Four Seasons and being approached by one of the Brothers who taught at the school.

"We will have tryouts soon for the 5th and 6th grade team, hope to see you there!" I felt like a rising star. It is always special for a young kid to be singled out by a coach.

We reached Third Avenue. Two topics immediately surfaced. Two topics of monumental importance, both then and now. Pizza and music. Truth be told, there is no pizza as good as New York pizza. And equally as true, the transition heard in music from 1959 to 1969 was astounding.

"Ma, its Friday, I'm gonna have pizza right?" All the kids in the building were Catholic and therefore none of us could eat meat on Friday. Every Friday we would make our way down the block to one of the pizza joints. The older kids would do the ordering and then we would meander over to the jukebox.

"Play 'Peppermint Twist.'"

"No, play 'Up on the Roof.'"

"Oh look, there's 'Speedy Gonzalez' by Pat Boone."

"Pizza ready yet?"

As the years went by the pizza remained the same, but the song choices did not. Ricky Nelson became Rick Nelson and eventually was booed off the stage at Madison Square Garden; Carole King, the writer, became Carole King, the singer-songwriter; Dylan went electric; the British invasion was commandeered by the Beatles; and the 1967 Summer of Love found fruition at Woodstock in 1969.

"Hey, did you hear? Paul's dead!"

The day had gotten away from us. We were not able to get to all of the landmarks that made an indelible impression on me. We had tickets for a Jethro Tull concert at Jones Beach. Procol Harum was opening. The concert was serendipitous to say the least, given the nostalgic day that had unfolded. The cab ride was expensive but a chance to relax and continue to share stories from our youth. Driving along the causeway we paid tribute to Sonny as we passed the toll booth where he was killed. Procol Harum opened with

"Conquistador" and closed with "A Whiter Shade of Pale." Tull opened with "Nothing is Easy" and closed with "Locomotive Breath." We called the same cabbie to come get us. I thanked my friend for spending the day with me and for reliving some of my childhood.

> *"Hey, wasn't that a great rendition Tull did of 'Living in the Past'?"*

Steve McNerney, 68, is a retired teacher and coach navigating life as an aspiring piano player and seeker of social justice.

HOT POCKETS AT THE APOCALYPSE

by CJ Green

IN LATE-DECEMBER OF 2013, I DROVE WITH COLLEGE FRIENDS from Charlottesville, Virginia, to Kansas City, Missouri, for a conference about the end of the world. We took I-64 West in my mother's Toyota Highlander, the dashboard of which was threatening that the anti-lock brakes had malfunctioned, but the regular brakes worked fine.

Because we were of the generation that believed everything valuable had to be witnessed, we recorded our adventure in a 30-minute video that still haunts the annals of YouTube. Skipping through it now, I spy snapshots of that time, and who we were: my banana-yellow puffer jacket, an old green afghan flung over the backseat, my passenger lolling his tongue like a wild animal. There were five of us, and we were all nineteen and twenty, and emphatically Christian. I was at the point where I celebrated every Jesus fish I saw on some stranger's bumper.

My primary concern was whether it would be enough of a road-trip. There had to be plenty of music, singalongs, and liberation. I got this expectation from movies probably. But there was a lot of silence, simply because there was a lot of time. For hours we wound through the mountains, rising and falling with the gradient of West Virginia. Over the course of Kentucky, the gnarled trees and rocky bluffs gave way to flat plains of wheat and corn. The sunset seemed to last longer than it usually did, either because I was driving blindly into it, or because we were crossing time zones at 80 miles per hour. I don't know if that makes sense.

We nearly ran out of gas somewhere in Illinois or Indiana, then crashed in a hotel, all in one room, and watched a show where a man was setting the world record for the amount of time spent in a tub of ice with only his head exposed.

The next day: back on the road. We stopped in St. Louis and ascended the Arch. The closer we drew to Kansas City, the more doubtful we became that we should stop there: why not continue, we wondered, to the Rocky Mountains? To California? The long flatness of America ran in every direction. We decided to stick to the plan.

That afternoon, we arrived at a Comfort Inn in Kansas City. I'd made the reservation online, had lied and said there would be only two of us sleeping there, when in fact, two others joined once we got in, for a total of seven men in one room, some of us sleeping on the floor in between beds and outside the bathroom. At a supermarket, we had loaded up on Hot Pockets, a bag of eighty. We microwaved them in our hotel room for dinner. Pretty good deal, we thought. I was trying to read *The Silver Chair* by C.S. Lewis, but I kept falling asleep.

What I remember most about Kansas City was that, downtown, maybe a half-mile from the convention center, the streets were deserted. I mean completely. Windows were dark. There were empty car spaces along every street. That is, until we arrived at the convention center. There, thousands of people had gathered, as if they had descended from the sky. You might have thought you were in Times Square. Pedestrians crowded the streets, and protestors picketed the false prophets at the conference. Guards stood at the entranceway checking bags. We processed through security, and inside, the auditorium was the biggest room I had ever been in my life. The sheer vastness left me disoriented. I'm not sure I ever recovered.

⁂ ⁂ ⁂

Before signing up for the conference, which was free, I had researched it online. Across forums, the hosts had been accused of corruption and cult-like behavior. But I also knew that that was the Internet, which couldn't be trusted, and I wanted to see for myself.

The first night involved lots of music. Front and center was a woman who sang beneath long dreads and a headscarf. She had survived a vicious bout of cancer, I learned later, and the dreads represented her rebirth or her strength or something like that. On YouTube, we discovered that she had also recorded a song called, "People Get Ready (The Lion of the Tribe of Judah)." Scary is how I would describe that song, if not eerily Freudian. "He's coming," she whispers, referring to the return of Christ; "the Jewish man … he will come again …." At the conference, she had written a new song that went over pretty well with the crowd, so immediately after hitting the final note, she turned to the band and ordered, "Play it again!" So they did.

That night's sermon was incoherent. All I remember was that the preacher said, "Beloved twenty-somethings, I urge you to read biographies!" The conference leaders were eager to herald the apocalypse, and not figuratively. We were told that it was necessary to pray day and night for the return of the Lamb. Presenters seemed to have googled every Bible verse about the end-times and were projecting them on screens. They were selling Papa John's. One man stood onstage and began making whale noises. He said that if Jesus came back, "You'd blow up right where you were at!" He talked about the meaning of opposable thumbs. We left mid-sermon and went to Denny's. Their paper menus were Hobbit-themed, because that was the big movie of the season.

Back at the hotel we played a card game with a family who had flown in from Greece—for the conference, which they were loving, which amazed me. They were a little pushy, and I began to feel that they were wasting my time. I went back to our room for some alone time. I tried again to read *The Silver Chair* and again fell asleep. To this day I have never finished it. My friends found me asleep and tried to play some prank, but I can't remember what it was. I just remember, through my sleepy eyelids, spying their bright faces peering from around the wall.

For some reason, we went back to the conference for one final session, where the director made a plea for one million dollars. We put our friend's phone number in the offering plate. One of my comrades said, "I need to be free of this!" but couldn't get the plastic admission band off his wrist. At the hotel, with scissors, he sliced it in half.

On the drive back to Virginia, we listened to "Free Bird," all nine minutes of it, and posted the same friend's phone number in the window and beneath it, "Call me maybe." After that, we wrote affirmations for the passing cars—"You are awesome," said one. None of the drivers seemed to notice.

Going to that conference had been like hiking for miles to an overlook you have only heard about. When you get there, what awaits is not a vista but a rock with a slug on it. It's so grotesque you stand there and study it, but soon you turn and leave, because there really is nothing to learn. Which perhaps indicates the true moral of this story: that is, how far twenty-year-old men would travel toward something they know nothing about. 2,000 miles precisely.

We returned to our college house at 11 P.M. on December 31. Everyone was too sick of one another to stick around and ring in the New Year. We retreated to our separate cars, and returned to our parents' homes. Mine lived two hours away, and I drove there alone. I was hungry. I pulled into McDonald's and ordered two number twos with sweet and sour sauce and an Oreo McFlurry. The radio clock hit midnight as I was reaching for my order through the window.

CJ Green is 26 years old and works as the managing editor at Mockingbird (mbird.com). CJ lives with his wife, Maddy, in Charlottesville, Virginia.

EDSEL

by Bahlmann Abbot

IN THE FALL OF 1967 LARRY PISHNER'S EDSEL LOOKED AS good as it had when it rolled of the assembly line almost a decade earlier. Unlike the Ford Motor Company, Larry had not given up on the quirky model sedan and had taken care of the car like a new girlfriend. Chances are it may have been the only Edsel left in southern West Virginia. Larry must have felt somewhat honored when his good friends Steve Pilato and Doc Dillon suggested that he provide transportation for our band to play a dance in Gauley Bridge. And Steve thought it might be cool to arrive in style at the "big gig" even though it was just another high school dance. It was to be held in the basketball gym of Gauley Bridge High School after the football game. It was our first out of town gig.

The Edsel was a two-tone sedan, a beautiful turquoise body with a white roof and accent panels. It had a big trunk that would fit Steve's drum kit, along with the guitars, amps, and mic stands our little combo required. Steve and Doc were sophomores and my friend Charlie Mahan and I were both in the eighth grade. Charlie and I were novice guitar players at best but highly qualified to be in the band as we were probably the only two kids in Fayette County with electric guitars. So Steve and Doc recruited us. We called ourselves "Doc and the Interns," a name that Steve's mother had suggested one day when we were practicing in her dining room.

Doc had probably never walked in his life; he was born with a strut and a chip on both shoulders. He could be intimidating but as friendly as they come once you got to know him. Steve Pilato had the good looks and big pearly smile that his Italian ancestors must have passed down, along with a warm gift for gab. As sophomores they were nearly grown men whereas Charlie and I were still in that awkward stage of intermittent growth spurts, acne, and squawky voices. We weren't allowed to sing yet, but we were no doubt thrilled to be playing with the older guys and naïve enough that the prospect of playing in another town seemed like some incremental step to future stardom. Nevertheless, it had taken some effort to convince our parents that we were in safe hands going down to Gauley, especially after they found out our last gig had been at the "Three Js Club" where we were legally too young to be in the place.

The trip from Fayetteville to Gauley Bridge had always seemed like an adventure just by the terrain one had to cover. You first had to descend on Route 16 into the New River Gorge along Laurel Creek with its series of dramatic waterfalls, then cross the river at Cotton Hill Bridge. From there it's a few miles up to Chimney Corner where you merge onto Route 60, long known as the "Midland Trail." The trail is believed to have been originally carved into the rugged terrain of the mountain by buffalo and native peoples. Then in the 1790s George Washington ordered the trail cleared. It was later traveled by stage coaches and the soldiers of the Civil War. Now it was Doc and the Interns in Larry Pishner's Edsel.

The "trail" winds across Gauley Mountain in an unending series of big curves where you are alternately weaving into the mountain coves then outward to the rim where the awesome void of the river gorge feels like it might suck you out into it. The traffic on this road fell off dramatically once the turnpike to the west went in, mostly local traffic and shunpikers. For that reason it was not a stretch of road you would want to break down on. It was not unusual to see abandoned cars stripped of their removable parts. There was also the lingering tale of the "Mad Butcher," Fayette County's own serial killer who left sawed off body parts in bags discarded over the drop to the gorge. As you approach Gauley Bridge you descend closer to the level of the river where you are eventually looking across a wide pool created by the hydro dam at Glen Ferris, just below where the New and Gauley rivers meet.

My memory is that the older guys sat in the front seat of the Edsel leaving Charlie and me in the back with plenty of room to stretch out in this hillbilly limo. When we arrived at the high school gym we found our way from a lower gravel parking area up a back stair into the empty gym. The vice principal of the school, a rather tall and imposing woman pointed us to the area at one end of the court under the basket and backboard. No stage for Doc and the interns but at least we had arrived in style. We returned to the Edsel and after two trips hauling our equipment, we set up to play. Our sound check was simple, tune the guitars and make sure there was power to the amps.

Once the football game was over, kids started pouring into the gym, throwing their winter coats on the bleachers and bringing their loud outdoor chatter into the cavernous space. Whenever we had played in Fayetteville, friends would gather around us to shoot the shit, but here the kids kept a suspicious distance. After a short while there was nothing to do but to start playing. We probably opened up with a favorite standard at the time "Wooly Bully" by Sam the Sham and the Pharaohs. Most of our repertoire was three chord variations of this song or the infamous "Louie Louie." I think Doc particularly liked "Wooly" because the jerky rhythm gave him an opportunity to strut his stuff, "watch it now, watch it now." And Doc had taken to wearing what Steve called his poofy hat (picture the newspaper boy's hat) that added to his cocky stage presence.

After a few songs, the kids came in closer and most started dancing and it seemed we were in for a fun evening. But like most high school events there always seems to be some older kids hanging around the edges looking to relive their school days or just looking for trouble. Sure enough after our first set, Larry noticed a gang of four or five guys hanging off to the side staring us down and, not surprisingly, annoyed with Doc. As the evening went on, they would come and go through the back door to the parking lot undoubtedly taking their fill of whiskey or moonshine. They were close enough that we could occasionally catch a whiff.

We probably ended the evening with a slow dance, perhaps The Beatles "Mr. Moonlight." And as we packed up, we were relieved to see the gang had left the gym. There were a few Gauley kids hanging around talking to us but soon the gym was cleared out. We packed up and started carrying our stuff to the back stair. After Doc, I was the last one to enter the stairwell, and before I had gotten half way down the first flight I could smell the alcohol and hear yelling. When I made it to the lower level and turned the corner, there just outside the open doors was Doc with a snare drum under one arm, an amp under the other, and a six inch steel blade under his chin.

The guy standing behind Doc and holding the knife was spouting off in a drunken slur something about who the hell did Doc think he was coming down here to his town actin' like he owned the place. There were three or four of his cronies standing close in, one now wearing Doc's poofy hat. Larry, Steve, and Charlie were nowhere to be seen and I learned later they were watching this play out from the parking lot below. From where I was I could see no good options that weren't suicidal. I stood with equipment in hand expecting to witness my first murder.

Then from above I heard a door open and someone making their way down the concrete stair. From some merciful heaven the tall lady descended like a hero angel, turned the corner beside me, and after assessing the situation for a split second I heard her yell with a seasoned teacher's authority, "Scott Hill!" In his wobbly state it took a few seconds for the knife wielder to find who had yelled his name and once he focused in on the tall lady the blade slowly dropped away from Doc's neck. You got the feeling that he had heard his name called like that many times before.

As soon as Doc had broken away from his grip, he and I made our way through a gauntlet of guys standing around the Edsel in the parking lot. With my bandmates' help we got our equipment in the truck and jumped in the car. Glancing back toward the gym we could see another teacher had joined the tall angel lady in an effort to corral the Scott Hill gang. But down in the parking lot other guys were crowding around the Edsel expressing their opinions of us and making it difficult for Larry to back up and pull away. When Larry finally had a clear shot at the exit, he gunned it just as a rain of gravel and rocks pelted the Edsel from all sides. You could sense the pain that Larry was feeling and for a brief second he slowed as if he was contemplating circling back, maybe with the idea of running over someone, but Steve just yelled, "Go, man, go!" and we were gone. Thinking this thing might not be over we watched to see if any cars were pulling out to follow us, but after a minute we saw we were alone on the highway speeding along the river back toward the mountain. Doc and the guys were fuming and already plotting some kind of retribution. Scott Hill, who the hell was this guy, where did he live, should we find him tonight? Charlie and I lay low in the back seat feeling like maybe we had had enough excitement for the night.

As we pulled the grade up the mountain, cooler heads prevailed and at some point the now battered old Edsel fell silent as we weaved our way along the midland trail with the ghosts of buffalo, Indians, and Civil War soldiers.

Just outside Fayetteville Larry turned up the driveway to my house. From the trunk of the Edsel, I took my guitar and amp in hand and walked up through the dark yard onto the front porch. In the brightly lit living room I could see my mom and dad and my brothers waiting up for me. As I stood looking through the window, I paused and tried to think through how I was going to tell this story and ever be able to play music out again. Then I put my hand on the front door latch and felt the familiar click of it spring open.

Bahlmann Abbot is a native of Fayette County, West Virginia. He currently lives with his wife, Bliss, in Greenwood, Virginia, where he draws houses, writes songs, scratches dogs, and plays with grandchildren.

DISTANCE LEARNING

by John Watterson

IT WAS EARLY NOVEMBER, AND A FIERCE WINTER STORM was bearing down on Sioux Falls, South Dakota.

Out the window of my twin-engine commuter, I watched as North Central Airline workers sprayed deicer on the wings. Apparently we were to be the last flight taking off for Rapid City.

The year was 1974, and I was flying west to teach a history class for the University of South Dakota in far off Belle Fourche. Long before digital distance learning or ZOOM gatherings, I was headed to teach a far more primitive version. I would meet with the class that evening and thereafter would communicate with them by telecalls. Students would send me their written work in the mail rather than online.

The plane rose jerkily through the clouds, and then I settled in for the hour flight to Rapid City. There a student would meet me and drive to Belle Fourche. If I worried about the storm, I didn't need to. When we arrived at Rapid City, there was no snow. How lucky I was, so I thought, to have narrowly avoided the storm and then have landed on the far side of the snow.

I gave the class as planned, and then my student dropped me off at a motel in Rapid City. I got up early on Wednesday morning and prepared to go to the airport. Luckily, before I called a taxi, I found out that my plane would not be flying. The Sioux Falls airport was snowed in.

After spending a day away from my family and classes, I was certain that I would be flying the next day. No such luck. I was still snowed out of eastern South Dakota, isolated in Rapid City. When the same thing happened on Friday, I decided to break out of quarantine. I would hitchhike the three hundred miles to Sioux Falls, retrieve my car, and drive sixty miles home to Vermillion. Pluckily, I walked to the highway outside the motel and stuck out my thumb. I had not hitchhiked since college, but I was determined to get home.

To my surprise, the first car that passed me stopped. The guy was driving to Sioux Falls, albeit indirectly, because Mr. Farragher was a feed and seed salesman who needed to stop and see customers on the way. (He later told me he stopped for me because he had forgotten to pay his motel bill and he thought I was sent from the motel.)

As it turned out, Mr. Farragher made only a single call, at a farm not far off I 90. I remember that the farmer had an odd pastime. He had captured a pregnant bobcat ("Bobby") and now Bobby had the run of his house. Bobby's children were housed in cages outside. Here was another surprise on what was becoming a surreal road trip.

Still no snow. But upon reaching the Missouri River on I 90, suddenly the mounds of snow loomed on either side. By nightfall, we reached the Sioux Falls Airport. I should have known. Not only was my car's battery dead, but the car was barely visible, covered by a massive snow drift. I would not be driving the sixty miles to Vermillion where my wife and twin daughters awaited me.

Another night in a dreary motel? Not this time; Mr. Farragher invited me to stay overnight at his house. That evening we drank martinis and dined on frozen dinners.

On Saturday morning, my benefactor drove me to the bus terminal where after two hours I would be back in Vermillion. I would deal with my car on Monday.

I never hitchhiked again.

* * *

Note: How do I remember Mr. Farragher's name after all this time? My Watterson ancestors hailed from the Isle of Man in the Irish Sea, not far from Liverpool, United Kingdom. I happened to know Manx names like Farragher. Sometime during that road trip I asked him if he was Manx. He looked at me blankly. "What's Manx?" When I explained about the Isle of Man, he recalled that his grandfather came from Man. Here it was another symmetry. One Manx descendant unknowingly rescuing his fellow countryman. So the name Farragher is etched in my memory.

John Watterson is retired from college teaching, most recently as an adjunct at James Madison University. He is the author of *College Football, History, Spectacle, Controversy* and *The Games Presidents Play*. He lives in the Charlottesville area.

JUNIOR BROWN'S PORCH

by Francis Eugene Wood

SOMEWHERE ALONG THE WAY DURING MY SENIOR year in high school I set upon the idea that five days of school per week was just not for me. Of course, these days there are proponents of the four-day school week and their arguments make perfect sense to me. But, where were they back then? No matter. I worked it out for myself and even had a verbal agreement with a forward-thinking assistant administrator (name withheld out of admiration and privacy) that as long as my grades did not suffer there would be no repercussions. So, I worked hard enough academically to keep my end of the bargain while savoring my "day off" per week for the mere enjoyment of exploration and pursuing life ambitions.

I have always had many interests, so a day of leisure appealed to me in so many ways. I could spend a day playing my guitar and writing songs or figuring out the chords to someone else's tunes. I could go hunting or fishing in season. I wrote quite a bit of poetry on occasion during those days off when I was in a reflective mood. Or, perhaps I might have decided to take a hike in the deep woods somewhere in an area where no one would question why a seventeen-year-old boy was out and about and not in school during a weekday. That was the key to my freedom, of course. Keeping a low profile and moving through wilderness or other obscure areas.

As you might imagine, road trips were to my liking in those days when wandering about was quite my sport. I drove a 1968 Camaro. It was a yellow beauty with black vinyl top and bucket seats. Gas was cheap and the road was an open invitation for me to roam and explore. I had moved to Farmville, Virginia, in 1971 and a year later was just realizing that this place in the heart of the state was the perfect base when setting out to parts unknown. I could be in the Blue Ridge mountains within an hour from my front door or on the coast in two and a half hours and back home for supper. I cannot deny that life was good!

One Friday morning in early October I arose with the thought that a day in the mountains would be to my liking. I knew that apples were in, and I was sure that my mother would be pleased if I happened to bring home a basket of some of those red delicious ones fresh out of the orchard. I could tell her that I went out to Boatwright's Orchard a few miles from our house and picked them up. Mom was working at the Longwood College library then and my dad was out of the house early with his job at Virginia Power. I left for school, so to speak, at my regular time (no, my parents were not aware of my four day school week). I hit the road at around 7:15 A.M. heading north up Route 15. It was a marvelous day when I turned left onto Route 60 and headed west. I could see the Blue Ridge in the distance and felt giddy with anticipation as I cut across and made my way over to Route 29 towards Lovingston.

The sky was cloudless as I came upon Route 29 and turned left towards Lynchburg. But, Lynchburg was not my destination. Too many people, you see. A few miles on 29 and I took a right turn onto Route 56. I was about two miles down 56 and according to a sign about a mile from Saunders Brothers Orchard when I decided to turn off onto a numbered road. There was no reason for it other than my own curiosity. I have always been bent that way. And, in this case I am so glad for it.

The neat little board and batten house was set back off the road a bit, but I saw it in time to study it from the road for a few seconds before I came to a complete stop. It was not the house that caused my pause, but the sight of a man sitting on the front porch with a guitar cradled in his arms. I rolled down my window and listened. It did not take me long to recognize the tune he was playing and singing. I pulled into the narrow driveway and eased my car up to the house.

When I opened my car door and stepped out the man stopped playing. I walked over to his front porch and said, "I saw you playing and when I rolled down my window to listen, I heard 'Hoochie Coochie Man.'" I smiled and stood at the bottom of his porch steps.

"You know Muddy Waters?" the man asked me. He rested his right hand atop his instrument which I saw was an ancient Gibson flattop. I could see it had been well used.

"I know his music," I replied. I pointed to a vacant slat-back chair and raised a brow. The man motioned for me to take a seat. I did. "You play it well," I told him as I sat down.

The man let go a toothy smile and I saw he did not have but a few in his mouth. He began playing "I Feel Like Going Home." He knew the blues. There was no doubt about that. I listened intently, leaned back in my chair.

When he finished the song he looked at me and said, "I'm Junior Brown. Come up from Memphis working the orchards with my wife and brother and his wife. They're out working now but I fell off the back of a wagon day before yesterday and wrenched my back." He looked at me but did not ask who I was or what I was doing.

So, I volunteered my name and told him I was taking a break from school. "You know any Robert Johnson tunes?" I asked him.

Without a word he launched into Johnson's "Terraplane Blues." I knew then for sure that I had happened upon the real deal with Junior Brown. He must have seen me eyeing the beat-up cigar box three-string propped against the front door frame because after he finished the song he laid his guitar down on the worn floorboards and pulled the instrument onto his lap. "You ever played one of these?" he asked me while tuning it.

"Never have," I confessed, "but, I have seen them in pictures and wondered how they are tuned." I leaned forward and watched Junior closely. "Is that an open tuning?"

He nodded his head. "Sure is. Open G. See here, it's G D G." He had it tuned in seconds. "There's some other tunings, but this is the one I use most times."

I listened as he played and sang Johnson's "Cross Road Blues." It was loud and raw and I was thinking this guy should be on a stage somewhere. But the front porch was his stage and it seemed to please him that a stranger was interested enough to sit and listen. He followed with "I Believe I'll Dust My Broom" on his flat top and then went back to Muddy Waters for "Rolling Stone" and "I Can't Be Satisfied."

I applauded him and said, "You certainly know how to play the blues!"

He laughed aloud and told me that he could play just about any type song. He liked George Jones, telling me that George had "white man's soul." Then he serenaded me with "She Thinks I Still Care." I was impressed to say the least. It's not every day one comes upon a self-taught maestro of common instruments who can play so well you just know they missed the boat to fame and fortune. Junior was that for me. I stayed on his porch for an hour or so just listening to him playing and singing. He even performed "Hound Dog," but it was nothing like Elvis. He said Elvis "stole that one."

Finally, I rose to leave and thanked him for the porch concert. I told him he should do some recording. But, he told me, "I ain't got no time or money for that. Besides, I play my best right here."

As I was stepping off the porch Junior said, "I worked for a boss man once over at Boatwright's whose name was Wood." He paused as if he was reaching far back into his memory. "Henry was his first name. Henry Wood."

I turned and looked at Junior. I think that was when I tried to figure his age for the first time. "That was my grandfather." My dad's father had worked at the orchard for several years as a foreman. It must have been in the late '30s and early '40s. "He's living in Farmville now. He moved his family there in the late '40s," I told him.

Junior threw back his head and laughed. "You tell Mister Wood that you run into Junior Brown, son." He slapped the top of his guitar and peered at me with his bloodshot eyes. "I thought there was something familiar about you," he said.

"I'll tell him," I promised. "Will you be here long?" I asked.

Junior shook his head and answered, "Oh, no. We'll be moving on soon as the picking is over."

I left and went up the road to Saunders where I purchased a small basket of apples for my mom. Another hour and I was home again. I spent the rest of the day in my bedroom trying to play "Hoochie Coochie Man" on my guitar the way I had seen and heard Junior perform it.

That little road trip back in 1972 is golden to me now as I think about it. Mom made the most delicious cobbler with the apples I brought home. And, I received an education in the blues you cannot get while sitting in a classroom. I guess you could call it a front porch education.

I told my grandfather about meeting Junior over in Nelson County. And he told me that he did remember a young man named Junior who played and sang for the fruit pickers during lunch breaks and at the end of the workdays when he was a foreman at Boatwright's Orchard. "He was a good worker, but a better guitar player." That was my grandfather's memory of Junior. Mine will always be of him playing and singing the blues on that front porch.

I never saw or heard of Junior Brown again after that road trip into the mountains. But I'll never forget him.

Francis Wood is President and GM of Colonial Broadcasting Company, Inc. (WFLO AM/FM Radio) in Farmville, Virginia. He is also an author and President of Tip-of-the-Moon Publishing Company. He lives with his wife, Chris, in Buckingham County, Virginia.

On Down the Line

by Dave Krovetz

Me and my old lady
Left town last year
Just about summer time
Grabbed keys to the pickup
Gassed her up
And rolled on down the line

Took a bottle of Bud
Another of Jack
An old hound dog called Joad
With Prine on 8-track
Singin' get a little Jesus
We headed down the west-
bound road

We traveled hard
And we traveled far
Running just to run
Didn't stop
'til we found ourselves
In the land of the midnight sun

Kept the pedal to the metal
Through Sioux Falls city
'til the mirrors showed the
Great Divide
The rhythm of the road
Played a song in our heads
A traveler's lullaby

We settled down
Up Klondike way
By a river clear and cold
Near the tailings of
A miner's dream
Where the sunlight felt like gold

We traveled hard
And we traveled far
Running just to run
And didn't stop
'til we found ourselves
In the land of the midnight sun

Yeah me and the old lady
Left town the other day
Just about supper time
Looking for a place
Called Paradise
Somewhere on down the line

We traveled hard
And we traveled far
Running just to run
Didn't stop
'til we found ourselves
In the land of the midnight sun

ON DOWN THE LINE: THE BACKSTORY

by Dave Krovetz

IN JUNE OF 1988, NATALIE AND I SOLD OUR HOUSE AND most of our possessions. We loaded what remained into the back of a U-Haul and began the process of moving from Charlottesville to Bellingham, Washington. I was to drive the truck cross-country accompanied by my faithful retriever, Goldie, while Natalie remained on the east coast with our daughter, Tess. Upon my return, the three of us would make our way west together.

The U-Haul truck we were so busily loading—and that would be my mobile home for three days—was not the truck we had reserved. The truck we were promised was shiny and new, ran like a top, and was perfectly suited for a cross-country trip. This version was a true beater long past its prime, barely suitable for driving across town. But somehow this was the truck we were stuck with. Packing complete, I fired up the truck and Goldie and I headed westward. Little did I know it then, but those first few hours on the road were my last moments of sanity for the three long days we allotted for my trip. I had return airline tickets for four days hence.

By the time we hit West Virginia, Interstate 64 had morphed from a modern four-lane into a narrow, twisting mountain byway. Already the truck was noisy, stinking hot, and uncomfortable. Clearly very little remained of its original suspension. Steering required an exhausting level of attention to the road and a never-ending series of course corrections; the wheel had far more free-play than directional-control. Top speed—with a good tailwind and on a downhill run—

was perhaps 65 miles per hour. In the mountains of West Virginia, 50 mph was only an unrealistic aspiration. I began to realize that we were in for a very long, strange trip.

As evening fell, we crossed into Indiana where we soon encountered a line of severe thunderstorms. By full darkness the storms had grown in intensity and the rain fell in sheets. Soon the windshield began to leak; at first as a constant drip, but around midnight as a steady stream whose terminus was somewhere inside the dashboard. And inside that dashboard, the rainwater inevitably found the truck's electrics; not surprisingly, we lost our headlights. Driving down an interstate highway in heavy rain and pitch-black night with no headlights, all while trying to see far enough ahead to spot an exit off said interstate—this was a formula for disaster. Ours took the form of a muddy ditch alongside a not-so-visible exit ramp. Leaving the truck behind, we hoofed it to a gas station to call for a wrecker. Several hours and too many tow-truck dollars later, we were back on the road. Night number one held no sleep.

Day two started off just fine. The weather was clear. The road was straight. We made decent time. Although I was tired, the trip felt doable. That all changed mid-morning. Our truck was parked on the highway's shoulder and I was talking to a Missouri State Trooper. Seeing the truck's meanderings—and assuming he had another drunk to deal with—he'd pulled us over. As per the man's instruction, I walked the line. He questioned me at length about where I was going and why. He inspected the cab. He inspected the suspiciously padlocked cargo box. Only after he felt the play in the steering wheel did he accept my explanation and send us off with a final admonition: drink a lot of coffee.

By afternoon we reached Sioux Falls. There a U-Haul mechanic repaired the electrics, restored the headlights, and opined that our truck would not make it to Bellingham. However, as they had no replacement truck on offer, we got back in the cab and continued on our way.

From South Dakota we crossed into Montana and began to labor up the eastern slope of the Rockies. Halfway up, we reached

Big Timber, Montana, where, with the temperature gauge pegged on red and the radiator boiling over, I was forced to stop. Big Timber was no more than a gravel cross-roads featuring one streetlight, a tiny post office, and a payphone—from which I called for some U-Haul "road-side assistance." Our road-side assistant finally arrived at 2 A.M., after hitchhiking for the last leg of his drive. His truck—a U-Haul vehicle, of course—had died just past Billings. In all fairness, I'd called for help at 11 P.M. And Big Timber was in the middle of absolutely nowhere.

One new thermostat and a radiator hose later, the truck was ready to roll, but not before my erstwhile road-side assistant added his two cents: noting the condition of the truck's tires (dry-rotted), he opined I'd be lucky to make it to Bellingham. With no spare and no choice, we headed west. Night number two, sleepless.

Early on the morning of day number three Goldie and I crossed the Continental Divide, drove through northern Idaho, and dropped into the state of Washington. Hours later and without further excitement we reached the outskirts of Bellingham. Having just covered 3,300 miles in 72 hours, I was predictably disoriented and foggy-headed. For one last time, I sought out a payphone, this time to call Anita, a Bellingham friend. Anita arrived, we caravanned to a storage garage, and together emptied the truck. I left Goldie to board at a kennel until our return in two weeks time. After gleefully returning the truck to a U-Haul dealer, Anita drove me down state to Seattle where I caught my plane home. Just as planned. Piece of cake.

I did not open my eyes until the plane touched down back east.

Dave Krovetz is a mathematician and teacher, builder and woodworker, musician of sorts, husband, dad, and granddad.

SNAPSHOTS FROM A WEST COAST ROAD TRIP

by Bill Dunnington

WHEN I WAS 26 (THAT WOULD BE IN THE LAST century), I decided to drive to the West Coast, travel and camp one summer between teaching years. I fixed up my Chevy pickup truck to cook and sleep in—and signed up to attend a three-week course in La Jolla, California, that started in early June.

The plan was to go out the southern route—stop to visit friends in Santa Fe—then on to La Jolla—then, over the summer, slowly up to Vancouver—back through Canada—and back to school by late August. Doing my drifting.

The big idea was to paddle my canoe in many places along the way. I left from the school where I was teaching in Kents Hill, Maine, drove first to Eastport and put in there for a sunrise paddle at the eastern-most point of the United States. The notion involved an eventual sunset paddle in La Jolla, so I could claim a true sunrise-east, sunset-west paddle adventure.

Oklahoma, west Texas, eastern New Mexico was a wasteland—flat, litter everywhere, no water anywhere. Pedal-to-the-floor, anxious to see friends in Santa Fe. But, the "Land of Enchantment" truly comes alive with sunsets.

Terrific visit to Taos with my photographer friend. Some great hash on the drive up from Santa Fe led us to seek munchies and beer in a grocery store. Terrific music was playing in the store; just had to tap the toes, shuffle a little. Suddenly there came a voice over the loudspeaker: "There will be no dancing in the aisles!" OK, already. So we left, picnicked and paddled some of the Rio Grande, and, of course, I stayed too long visiting—left just one day to drive from Santa Fe to La Jolla, 839 miles.

It was 90 degrees by 7 A.M. No AC. Across New Mexico into Arizona. Have to stop at the Grand Canyon ... not to paddle, but just to see it somehow. Hey, there's a sign: Piper cub flights down the canyon—one hour, $25. The pilot was just back from flying helicopters in Vietnam. A tiny plane covering a huge hole in the ground. Awe-inspiring views. Someday, I'd like to go back and do the long trip down the river—not in a canoe.

Back on the road. Driving in boxers. Arm out the window getting sunburned. Across Death Valley. Hot. Turned southwest at Bakersfield. Hot. Seriously hot. Can't wait to get that canoe in the Pacific. Did I mention hot?

The coastal highway north of La Jolla goes along the edge of high cliffs with occasional great views of all that cool Pacific water, but no clear way to get down to it. Until, suddenly, not on the map, there's a pull over and a ravine down to the ocean. Jump into my trunks, and with the canoe on my head, I head down this ravine. Can't wait to cool off. After quite the walk, I'm on flat sand, can hear the ocean—but can't see it yet because of a very wide beach, and the canoe over my head.

Suddenly, out of my right-side field of vision, two people appear—a young man and young woman. Their heads were not visible because of the canoe—but both in their birthday suits, and in a condition of, shall I say, excitement. They walked 10 feet in front of me, right to left. I hear noises up the beach to the right, so I lift up the canoe to take a look.

There are hundreds of people. Playing volleyball. Hang gliding off the cliffs. Throwing a football. Surfing. Body surfing. Tanning. Not a stitch of clothing anywhere. And here I am—wearing a bathing suit with a canoe over my head. "Welcome to California," I thought. Welcome to Black's Beach, actually. Took a little getting used to.

Paddling out though Pacific surf was a challenge. But the cool water was delicious and the sunset was stunning.

The program in La Jolla was at the Carl Rogers Institute. My father had given me Rogers' book, *On Becoming a Person*, and it opened a world of insights. The program was for people interested in learning to facilitate personal growth groups, a career I was considering. As it turns out, I have never actually led any of those groups, but I learned a ton about people and myself at a formative time and the experience has served me well all my life. And there was lots of driving time ahead to reflect on learnings, priorities, hopes and intentions.

In San Francisco, I bought two large slabs of redwood burl—4 inches thick, 48 inches plus cross, free edge, with vibrant grain to make into tables. (And slept on them the rest of the trip.) I still have them—now, two tables. At Fisherman's Wharf, I befriended a guy in a gorilla suit playing a trumpet.

The east is quaint, but the west is awesome. The redwoods. Backpacking and fly fishing in Tuolumne Meadows. Mount Shasta climb. Coos Bay. Over to Bend. Back to the Oregon coast. Portland. The Columbia River. The Washington coast. Olympic. Seattle. Vancouver. The San Juan Islands. Victoria. East to visit friends in Kamloops, British Columbia. Paddled across Lake Moraine in Banff. Regina—talk about flat. North shore of Superior. Lake of the Woods. Georgian Bay. Into the muskeg. Thousand Islands. The Saint Lawrence. Home stop in Lake Champlain. Trip of a life.

Bill Dunnington lives in Vermont on the shores of Lake Champlain.
He is "kinda sorta" retired.

UTAH

by Zack Verham

WE SQUINTED AND SHIELDED OUR EYES AGAINST the sharp glare of the sun as we scanned the pickup queue outside of the Salt Lake City airport, looking for my old college housemate's white SUV among the dust-covered cars that moved in and out of the loading zone like judicious worker ants. My wife and I had flown out to meet him and a second couple—another UVA roommate and his spouse—for a whirlwind tour of the Beehive State, and we planned to visit every national park in Utah over the course of one short week. This was perhaps a little overzealous, but we were all still recently-minted UVA alumni with lots of energy and the ability to operate with minimal sleep still etched into our DNA from all-nighters and college shenanigans, so it felt like the only rational choice. If we were in Utah, we might as well make the most of it, right?

We spotted our ride, hauled our bags through the dry heat of the western desert, opened up the trunk to wide grins and loud celebration, and kicked off a reunion on the other side of the country that none of us would have ever anticipated or dreamed of while we were students just a few short years ago.

There is much that I could wax poetic about regarding the trip itself. The afternoons spent peering out of the passenger-side window, our now-Utah-native guide driving us through endless expanses of flat shrublands which, in the distance, were violently ripped into clear blue sky by the largest mountains I have ever seen. The sting of small scrapes and cuts on our hands and knees as we climbed along dusty trails which were carved out of cliff faces worn down by rivers and creeks, a process that had started in some primordial time from the distant past and would continue long after we were gone. The feeling of relief when, after being battered about by the sweltering sun, we found a cool emerald pool nestled in a canyon alcove and took our shoes off to feel the warm desert sand between our toes as we splashed into the frigid water shaded by the cliffs above.

Staring across endless expanses of canyon and cliff face in dusk, eyes lost in the swirling infinite pattern of canyon walls that doubled back and around and back again, then looking up to see the clear brightness of the Milky Way reflected inadequately by the speck of light in the far distance illuminating some small town—all of these images will stick with me for the rest of my life. But they aren't why I hold my trip to Utah so close and dear to my heart.

We packed up one morning to see the bane of any road trip: a lopsided tire, punctured by a deformed nail. This was, to put it mildly, unfortunate, because we were literally in the middle of nowhere, having just spent the night in an "airbnb" which appeared to be a repurposed storage unit, and our overzealous schedule meant we had minimal flexibility in our travel time. The situation transitioned from unfortunate to tragic, however, when we attempted to remove the lug nuts to put on our spare and accidentally ripped the bolts off of the chassis of the SUV. Oops. So it was in a relatively dire situation that we limped to the nearest mechanic in a tourist trap nearby and walked half a mile down the highway to a small combination pizzeria/coffee shop to wait on the repairs. We had eaten some decent Utah 'za there the night before, but were obviously not expecting to spend six hours in the same dining room the subsequent day.

If I was by myself, or even with a group of acquaintances, this could easily have dampened the mood of the whole day. Most of our optimal daytime was wasted in a strange coffee shop, getting caffeine headaches and waiting on a large mechanic bill while the wild west was out there for us to explore and experience. Yeesh.

But the whole point of the trip was never really about the experiences and the sights and the sounds, was it?

Since the muggy June day in Virginia when I shook the hand of my dean and received my diploma, I've always felt no small amount of existential dread regarding what would happen to those friendships after we entered the big, wide world of careers and property taxes and medical insurance. Almost every older adult in my life has stories of wonderful friends from young adulthood that they "lost track of over the years." In all honesty I have been terrified of that grim eventuality since my senior year—my college friends have their handwriting in the most important chapters of my life, and the idea of "losing track" of them felt so awful. It still does.

But looking back on the time we spent in that tourist trap coffee shop, reading or laughing or playing games or reminiscing about the pranks we pulled in undergrad, I know now that there will always be space for them in my life—even if they move from the verdant humidity of Virginia to the dusty mountains of Utah. I know that those friendships are much more important than the memory of any particularly big mountain or canyon I took a picture of, and because my companions were just as happy sitting around drinking coffee with me as they would have been out in the desert, collecting "experiences," I know that they felt the same way, too.

Of course, the week ended, and we all parted ways and went back to our respective lives—distinct in many ways from the lives that had been braided together during our college years. But that day in the coffee shop brings me more comfort than I can really express, and I will always be thankful for my travels across the state of Utah with some of my closest friends, seeing mountains and ripping bolts off of my college housemate's SUV.

Zack Verham and his wife, Erin, are from Crozet, Virginia. They love living near the mountains with their Corgi puppy, Sesame.

ROAD TRIP

by John R. Schoonover

IN 1966, OBSERVING NORMAL PREPARATIONS THAT preceded most road trips from Charlottesville, fraternity brother Rusty Adams and I made a phone call for dates, jumped into my '61 Corvette, and took off for Madison Women's college in Harrisonburg, Virginia. Renamed James Madison University in 1977, it was one of several popular women's institutions, among them: Sweet Briar, Hollins, Mary Baldwin, and Mary Washington College. Mid week road trips, often spontaneous, were a respite from the all-male camaraderie at UVA. No doubt Rusty and I included a six-pack of roadies. Coat and tie, of course. No Google Maps back then, which today describes a trip to James Madison as two hours and twenty minutes. I guess it didn't matter to us. Leaving Charlottesville for these road trips, you either went 29 North and South or 250 East and West. Getting lost was never an option. Our homing pigeon instincts kicked in. Good thing, because the return trip on dark, single lane roads, mildly inebriated, or worse yet, drunk, left little to be desired. No room for error. Often, I confess, the driver home remained a mystery the next day.

My somewhat cloudy memory of this particular trip, even to this day, is punctuated by the drive north on 29, then a left on 33, as the road ascends through Shenandoah National Park, then gently down to another rise and fall, Massanutten Mountain. Unfortunately, early along Route 33, Carl Sandburg's fog "on little cat feet" enveloped the car. Undeterred, I posted Rusty on the hood of the car, not unlike the lookout for the icebergs on *Titanic*. We limped along with a visibility of three to five feet for a considerable time, at which point my memory fails me entirely. No doubt our eventual arrival involved taking dates to the local pub, a few pitchers of beer, and a long, long drive home, one or the other us steering the way.

I am sad to report we buried Rusty, my good friend and Elmo, a couple years ago in Savannah, but at least we made it over Massanutten Mountain.

John R. Schoonover graduated from St. Andrew's School in 1963, then the University of Virginia in 1967. Since 1969, he has served as President and Curator of Schoonover Studios Ltd. John co-edited the *Frank E. Schoonover Catalogue Raisonné* in 2009, and he is currently writing a book on Frank E. Schoonover's social documentary photography.

ROAD WEARY

by Tony Zentgraf

LOOKING OVER MY RIGHT SHOULDER, I TRACKED A Texas Leaguer from my second base position. I dove at the last minute, colliding with the centerfielder's left knee. That was in the bottom of the fourth inning in the first of a three game series in Johnson City, Tennessee. It was also my first night as a professional ball player and I stayed on the bench for the remainder of that game recovering from a slight concussion.

"Leave the driving to us" was Greyhound's slogan. I left Charlottesville late in the afternoon the day before heading southwest to Pulaski, Virginia. The outside temperature rose to 90 and the overcrowded bus was just a few degrees cooler, so the bus smelled of somebody sobering up, double knit butts, and left-over cigarettes. We meandered through tiny towns discarding and picking up passengers with no net loss of people. So when I arrived in Pulaski after hearing "Don't Go Breaking My Heart" for the sixth time that day, I was relieved to step onto the soft asphalt parking lot where I decided that Greyhound would not be a consideration for future travel.

A short cab drive landed me at Calfee Park, home of the Pulaski Phil-O's. The clubhouse fella met me at the locker room and told me to suit up and report to the dugout. Watching the game while partially recovering from Greyhound exhaust, I was called up to pinch hit in the bottom of the eighth. I had started the day without a contract while the Appalachian league finished its tenth day of play;

by 8 P.M. I had one, but still found myself wondering where I would sleep that night in this textile town.

The manager said that he would see me on the field at nine the next morning. I worked out for an hour at second base turning double plays and covering the bag on steals. I was a left-side infielder, third baseman, and totally unprepared when the manager told me I would be starting at second base that night in Johnson City. I thought I was going to ease into the team in my third base role, but as it turned out the second basemen ahead of me had failed to impress the manager during the opening days of the season. And there was a hot shot eighteen-year-old holding down my base.

We loaded onto a school bus just before noon for what would normally be a two hour trip, but because the school bus engine was governed to fifty-five mph we arrived in a dead sweat around 4:00 while Abba played on someone's transistor radio. We used commercial travel in the minor leagues too, so riding on a school bus wasn't always the mode, but sometimes the humid air in the high end buses was worse than air blowing your hat off in the back of a Pulaski County yellow bus during those midday heat stroke trips.

Games were over around 10:30. Relief from the heat, the manager, traveling scouts, the fans, and your batting average began at 11:00 with supper, alcohol, a couple of bong hits, an ongoing card game. We went to bed around 3 A.M. Because we needed to be at the field two and a half hours before game time, we had about fourteen hours to recover. We played every day but the longer rest period occurred once every three days—when we again loaded and unloaded our favorite mechanism of travel. We usually stayed on the road for at least nine games, a three game series in three small Virginia towns was the regular schedule.

Trying to get to the unassigned seats on the bus required some strategy. This is where the real game took place. Seats changed every trip as players became major leaguers at seat choice. You didn't want to sit too close to the coaches in the front, nor too far in the back where the hungover or hallucinating hid from authority and the noonday sun. The middle was prime but popular with a lot of competition; you wanted to be alone in a single seat to spread out, all the time you were sweating and wondering how you were going to make it over the next mountain. Then the smell of heated brakes found its way through your window.

The minor league bus experience had little camaraderie. Staying cool was a problem, the smells did not help with digesting your stomach contents, and self improvement like reading or writing were impossible because of the constant feeling that the bus body was not connected to the chassis. Pulaski to Johnson City, Elizabethton, Kingsport, Bristol, and back to our home base lasted thirteen days. That was my introduction to minor league travel.

Some of my teammates never gave minor league travel a thought. They accepted the noise, smells, heat, and lack of team spirit because they were there to play baseball. They came from poor countries, had no support or hope, but they played hard, sent money home, and couldn't wait to prove that they should move up. My college spring break trips in a souped up university bus that was our second home made me think that I had already made it to the 'show' and earned some comforts. Maybe I should have settled into those bus seats, enjoyed the ride and left the driving to them, while I spent my time getting better at second base—where they thought I could help the team.

Tony Zentgraf has been a Health/PE teacher at Burley Middle School for the last twenty-three years. He has coached baseball, worked as a farmer, formerly served as the executive director of Camp Holiday Trails, and owned a summer camp called Camp Wahoo. Tony enjoys gardening, exercise, music, naps, and especially his best buddy, Kathy.

A FEW CUPS OF COFFEE

by Paul Erb

FIND YOUR FRIENDS AGAIN. FACE TO FACE. IT'S WORTH IT.

Not long before the summer of 2015, I had just lost my two closest friends. Then my father died. So it all snapped into place for me, and I decided to go back to teaching. In the summer between my last day with the financial statements and my first day back with e e cummings, I fitted out my Subaru Forester with half-inch Grade A plywood boards to sleep on and coolers to eat from and a sleeping bag to sleep in, on a mission to see old friends and former students living dotted across America. Inspired by Facebook, I had decided, at 59, not to let their faces turn all digital. And after fifteen years of business life, it was time.

I met each over a cup of coffee, asking each the same three questions: "What's your job now?" "What's your life's work?" "How did your education help you answer those two questions?" In St. Louis, former student Marisa's an art professor; in Lawrence, cycling buddy Walter warehouses rare academic books; in Los Angeles, former student Franklin's a screenwriter; Emily ran a gap-year internship shop in San Francisco; Meredith's an architect in downtown Denver; Humphreys defends death-row inmates in Sacramento; Alice runs a fly-fishing outfit in Yellowstone; former love Caroline's husband glowered politely across the table at me in Missoula; Daryl lives for his kids; Dick remembers Roosevelt; Jim's still a Republican; Hillary remembers her essay about wolves;

Phil, who restores old buildings, remembers a teacher who didn't say much, but said what mattered; Peggy teaches physics for an administration that doesn't care; Cassandra teaches because she *does* care, because kids *matter*. Art teacher Caroline and marketer Kelly are pushing the world in opposite directions; but they love each other.

And the long time alone on the road was a chance to spend time with the spirits.

✳ ✳ ✳

Dear David,

Today I drove screaming out of the mountains and into the desert.

It didn't start out as screaming. I had just left Zion National Park's gorges—celebrate the homophone, if you like—and now I had the windows open wide coming down the interstate, and on either side the roadcuts showed naked and bony-dry the thrust-up geology of orange/ochre/yellow mud that once was placid lakebed. It used to be wet there.

These bent layers, folded and lithified, more or less barren now, sat there, so beautiful and fertile-promising while I flew by, that I could hardly keep my eyes on the winding road. I thought without words that if only enough rain could fall here, maybe ancient seeds long dried would sprout and tell their stories, and the whole friable landscape would be transformed and live again.

At turns I could see already in the flat sun the miraged highway path below, the way, the Dao, the *nothing* that would lead me on.

I was pushing 80. I had to shower in a Planet Fitness I'd targeted in Vegas and get to Los Angeles for the next cup of coffee. The park's magic, contemplative canyons—a proper home for a Delphic oracle—lay now behind me, and I had an interview to get to.

In the Subaru's CD slot I had Beethoven's 9th on, and here, in its own sweet time, came the Chorale. Conductor: Toscanini, and—get this—the NBC Symphony Orchestra! Who knew that

NBC ever had an orchestra? Reminds me of the Rockettes and all that fading New York stuff you showed me that time I visited you in your apartment on West 4th. Maybe NBC did more than sports and comedy, back in the day, when our fathers were young and virile and radio carried voices to farmers.

Me, I had sung the 9th back home, not so long ago, with Charlotte in the alto section. So I knew my tenor part. And I started singing it, windows open, to nobody. That's some full-throated freedom there. The volume high, and only the wind and the passing rocks to answer, I let the sound rip.

And then came the volcano. Remember those pictures Miss Turner showed us, that 4th-grade year we did the reports on nature? You and I, little scholars, did our joint report on sharks and barracudas, and she thought maybe we'd like to do something just as exciting about the Earth, and showed us the *World Book Encyclopedia*'s cutaway drawing of a brown mountain and the red-hot magma spurting up through its hidden core. It looked as if the whole Earth had something hot and exciting to give. Remember that?

As the sound came up my throat, yelling all those familiar pitches together with those NBC singers, and Charlotte now in New York with Sam, and you, wherever you are, not able, never, now, able to hear me; Lear said, *Why should a dog, a horse, a rat have life, and you no breath at all?*

Before long it was just wind and sobs and the road cuts, and here came the desert and the heat and the long stretch to Los Angeles, and Virginia far, far behind.

Love,
Paul

⁕ ⁕ ⁕

O David,
Who taught me
Not too long ago

That omicron's the little oh
And omega, big—
The joy of learning with you
So young was Heaven.

When now you come again in dreams
Always silent, ever warm,
Or through the easy gait
Of that tall bald guy I see there
Strolling Granite Avenue across
From this dusty bookstore
Not twenty yards from where our little feet
Carried us together home
After school talking idly of
God knows what,
I know that hot ancient thirst
That made a resurrection of mirage.

* * *

Dear Jim,

In 2015 heard you in Pike Place Market.

I don't know if you can remember those people you introduced me to in Seattle. When we took that trip together after graduation, hitchhiking from Washington to Washington, we slept on the floor with some friends of yours somewhere up near Green Lake. A couple among them needed a driver in August to help them haul a pair of cars back East.

I agreed to do that after you and I hitched on down the coast, two carefree young men—boys, really—among the famous trees. By the road I lamented the loss of forests, and vowed to reduce my paper consumption. "That's just an act of self-definition," I can still hear you saying. I never heard you lie, not once.

After we split up in Berkeley, you settling in with that hot love of yours, I went east to Yosemite, looped up back through Reno and Yellowstone and Idaho, to meet up with that ride-needing couple in Seattle, as we had prearranged. Remember back before mobiles, when we prearranged things? Your endorsement made them trust me, I guess. Thank you for that.

I don't think I ever told you that before I got back to Seattle, going west out of Spokane, after I'd been arrested in Oakland a week before for hitching on the freeway, I walked past the unambiguous No Hitchhiking sign on the on-ramp and vowed to take the first offer that came. I had to get to Seattle by nightfall.

The first car that stopped was a Rambler Ambassador. Tame enough. I threw in my pack, said thanks, and hopped into the front seat. We took off. On that long, long ride through the alternating deserts and orchards of eastern Washington, I learned with alarm that my ride was a pimp, that the car was stolen, and that her top speed was 98 when he had his foot to the floor and his butt was off the seat. I looked out the window at the unspeaking flatness and thought, "I'm going to die here."

But you know what? As you said to me once … sometimes the best a psychotherapist can do is help patients achieve a normal state of misery. He turned out to be a real person, a lot realer than some of those guys we knew in college; and he gave me a ride for free.

Things calmed down. I listened. He had family, and stories to tell. And when he let me off, shaken but alive, at Pike Place, the first thing I heard was a street musician, playing well, just like you. The sound of her violin string felt so alive, vibrating there in the air, that I took five precious dollars and dropped them in her open case.

Almost forty years later I went back to that corner in Pike Place, and felt you there, felt our whole history back again, humming in the vibration of a remembering string.

Love,
Paul

⁕ ⁕ ⁕

Elegy for a Misshapen Peach

I found you on a grocery shelf
Of odd-lot fruit, sequestered,
And with a little money made you mine.
Forgive me when I say
You were delicious
So sweet and so cold
And all I needed for breakfast.

You can tell your mother
(though she knows)
That your juice and your firm flesh
Sang praise of her branches
And of all the work
Of waiting and of flowering and of bearing love
In long anonymous irrigated rows.
For her I tossed your pit with vigor
Out the passenger-side window
Just to lie exactly by a California stream
In soil where the sun will shine
And your perfection shall be rememberéd.

Paul Erb was born and raised in Richmond, Virginia. He has two daughters. Since 1978 he has taught high-school English, with side trips to grad school in the '80s, to Capital One in the '00s, and as a school business manager in the '10's. He lives now with his wife in Orange, Virginia, where he teaches and coaches squash at Woodberry Forest School.

MEDITATION AT LAGUNITAS BREWERY

by Andrew Deloss Eaton

ALL THE NEW DRINKING IS ABOUT HOPS. IN THIS IT
resembles the old drinking. The idea that if an
object, a barrel of ale, for example, which carried
overseas is prone to stale, can be obscured by a
mask of floral scents, for instance, it has been
altogether changed. The font across my coaster
peels away, imitating either a wanted poster or
the burnt out hair and skin from a cattle
brand—in biodegradable paper and ink, it says
on the back—is neither, but rather a moody
signifier of them both. Or the notion that, since
industry is increasingly digital, forms of
physicality including labor even have become
nostalgic in as much as they are willed. By
some. We talked about it last month on
FaceTime and in the voice of my friend there
was a thin wire of spliced static, a tone almost
mechanical in the little speaker on my laptop.
After a while I understood my bandwidth needed
to be wider. There was a road I watched while
my father drove the brown pickup. Opening the
small triangle-shaped window, I would smell the

tangle of gravel and saltwater, feel surrounded
with presence, like darkness around a lit match. I
wanted to increase, I wanted to decrease, I
wanted to become him, I wanted never to
become him. Become, I say, since I am full of
movement. Particles of me are even moving
now, the article in the science magazine tells me
before I return it to the stack of them sitting on
the counter. Those street lamps at the peninsula,
a boardwalk the imagination follows until the
daydream turns its open sign to CLOSED. I hear
Citra and Cascade hops release vowels without
language in my throat. The server draws the
shade open on a pit bull who lifts its head.
Outside, a black star of smartphones on the
metal table pulsing: *listen, listen, listen.*

(after Robert Hass)

Andy Eaton was born in California and raised throughout the United States. He earned a PhD in English from the Seamus Heaney Centre for Poetry in Belfast, Northern Ireland and is a Henry Hoyns Fellow at the University of Virginia. The recipient of the 2017 Ploughshares Emerging Writer Award in Poetry, his poems appear in or are forthcoming from *Colorado Review*, *Cortland Review*, *Copper Nickel*, *IMAGE*, *Ploughshares*, *The Winter Anthology*, *The Yale Review*, and elsewhere.

MILES AND MILES

by Corky Schoonover

I STILL HAVE A LETTER THAT I WROTE TO MY FATHER DATED November 7, 1973, in which I wrote: "I made it back safe and sound from my greatest hitchhiking trip yet—3,100 miles in 4½ days." The journey, Berkeley, California, to Charlottesville, Virginia, capped a series of events that started in August.

I was at loose ends then; my mother had passed away unexpectedly in 1968 when I was 16 and my father was now seriously ill and remarried to a woman who kept me at bay. Dad had been perplexed when I dropped out of UVA in the fall of 1970 to be the drummer in an ill-fated rock 'n' roll band in Massachusetts. Still determined to play music, I had regrouped by saving to go to the Berklee College of Music in Boston but my first semester had just ended and I was broke with no prospects. After storing my few possessions with a friend, I headed back to Charlottesville, home to my heart. There I spent aimless end-of-summer days with friends playing backgammon, sneaking into the Farmington pool, and test-driving new cars at McGregor Motors on Main Street to pass time on rainy days. So when my friend Nancy asked about helping her drive to Boulder where she was starting college I thought, why not? I had little money, no idea how long I would be gone, and no idea how I would get back; it seemed like a no-brainer!

Five of us—Nancy, Jim, Johnny, Karen, and I—powered straight through on Route 70, fueled in part by vodka mixed with Clamato juice. In the impossibly flat land of Kansas, a full-sky evening lightning storm and, later, my first sight of the Rocky Mountains were awe-inspiring. I may have been channeling a touch of Jack Kerouac or the Merry Pranksters but I was really feeling the euphoria of being "on the road." I'd left behind any obligations I had in Boston: no rent, no car, no homework—nothing. I would live by my wits.

In Boulder, Jim, Johnny, and I slept in Nancy's van for a week—think *The Three Stooges*. We watched Little Feat open for Leon Russell at the University of Colorado football stadium and then asked for loose change near a concession stand during Leon's set. I was already experienced at panhandling, mostly from stationing myself outside Fenway Park in Boston after home games. I always requested "exactly 18 cents" and hoped for (and frequently got) a quarter instead; a handful of quarters was actually worth something in those days. There were side trips to Denver to see Little Feat again and Dan Hicks and His Hot Licks. In Denver we also met three friends from Charlottesville who were driving to California and all hiked up Longs Peak in the Rocky Mountain National Park. On our "days off" we made it the 30 miles to Golden three times for the unlimited free beer after the tours at the Coors brewery. A not-so-successful venture was rushing the Sigma Nu house at UC posing as visiting brothers from UVA. We headed straight for the beer but were quickly surrounded and quizzed; it turns out that the Sigma Nu motto is not "Sigma Nu—what a zoo."

Following a very loose plan to reunite with our friends, Jim and I left Boulder to hitchhike to California by way of Las Vegas. I was also experienced at hitchhiking and always followed three rules: clean clothes, combed hair, and most importantly, a legible sign. Trust me when I say that $10 doesn't go far in Las Vegas; Jim and I spent a long time feigning dropping coins into the slots in order to get the free drinks offered to active players. Our money went instead to Wonder bread and baked beans for the ride to California and we arrived late on a Saturday at our friend Dan's house with 13 cents between us. Dismayed, he quickly set down some rules: he would buy one six-pack of beer to share; treat us to breakfast in the morning at his restaurant, the Soup Kitchen on Telegraph Avenue; and he insisted on absolutely no panhandling in front of his restaurant.

We had our fun in Berkeley too. There was an Asleep at the Wheel show, a trip to Reyes Point on a foggy afternoon, a weekend at the annual (pot) Harvest Festival in Big Sur and three days at Yosemite. We also quickly became regulars at Dan's favorite neighborhood bar, Mike and Mary's, and even got used to watching Monday Night Football at 5:30 P.M.

At the same time, a sense of grind was beginning to encroach on my original euphoria at being totally footloose and fancy-free. The Flower Power days were long over and Telegraph Avenue was now packed with folks who were truly down-and-out, and competing for the same change I was. Overall, I was receiving but not really giving anything back. Having no real focus or goals was becoming increasingly uncomfortable. I realized that I still wanted to play music and somehow get back into Berklee. It was time to go. I needed to get back to the East Coast and hitchhiking seemed like my only choice. Having tapped all my West Coast resources, I contacted a friend in Boston who kindly sent me some money for the trip.

I left on a typical California day and if you've been there you know what I mean: sunny, a totally blue sky, and 80 degrees. I was confident and yet apprehensive as this trip would be 2,500 miles longer than my previous longest hike and would include multiple nights on the side of the road, no showers, and inconsistent meals at best. I've long since forgotten most of my rides but a few still stand out. In Reno, a man picked me up in a modified police cruiser. He boasted that he could outrun any patrol car and proved it by averaging 120 mph for the entire 520 miles to Salt Lake City. I was now in a very conservative area and had waist-length hair so I was on edge when a pickup with a gun rack stopped and offered me a ride in the bed. However, it proved to be one of my most pleasant rides as I enjoyed a beautiful fall night while relieved of the constant chit-chat that is a part of hitchhiking. Nearing Boulder I stopped for two nights to see Nancy and Johnny and then pushed on.

A couple gave me a lift right away and also generously shared their stash of Dexedrine. That streamlined the trip—no sleeping and little eating! I got stuck once as I explained in the letter to my father: "When you stand in one place for five and a half hours, which I did at a truck stop just this side of Kansas City, you begin to wonder if you'll ever make it." Two truckers rescued me, sharing funny stories and their tricks of the road for 150 miles. That boosted my spirits. I was starting to get excited with the end slowly coming into sight and feeling an increasing determination to rekindle my music career when I got back. I might remain on the margin of the US economy—and I did for six more years—but I would put one foot in front of the other going forward.

There was one scary moment when I was propositioned in the middle of the night by a man outside of Columbus, Ohio. Thankfully he acquiesced to my request to let me out then and there, in the middle of nowhere, so that he could move on. I didn't share that with my dad. Instead, I did note: "It was good to get into Pennsylvania where I finally caught up with the autumn I am used to." When I finally made it to Charlottesville I'd been awake for 56 straight hours and covered 1,620 miles on the second leg. I had done it!

* * *

I returned to another semester at Berklee and continue to play music to this day.

My father passed away two and a half years later never knowing that I would finally get my BA from UVA in 2012 (the 44-year plan!).

I only have one photo from the trip; it's a complimentary photo from Red Garter's Casino. I'm sitting in front of a slot machine in jeans and a paisley shirt holding a drink cup. It looks like a typical photo from a gambling junket but now you know the rest of the story.

Corky Schoonover retired two years ago after both a 12-year career as a full-time musician and a 30-year career as a sales manager at Crutchfield. He still plays music and also enjoys sports, gardening, reading, and traveling.

QUARTERS

by Chris Poe

A LACK OF SLEEP COMBINED WITH TOO MUCH BOURBON the night before made tying my shoes a chore as anxiety coursed through my body. This wasn't the garden variety angst I felt before some road trips … "have I packed well, will my alarm go off, have I misplaced my license?" My anxiety was born out of a sense of discomfort and fear. This was a road trip unlike any I'd ever taken before. It lacked the excitement of visiting new places, cultures and sights—although this trip surely would provide all that. This trip was to a place I'd never planned to visit and hoped never to return.

James and I had been friends for 30 years. We ran in the same circles, worked for the same non-profit out of college and later in the same professional field. While I had moved away from my hometown after college, he moved there, even in the very neighborhood where my parents still lived. Our paths crossed frequently, and I always left our times together feeling encouraged. In short, James was one of the most charismatic people I'd ever met. Tall, athletic, handsome with an extroverted relational motor that never lacked fuel. People were drawn to him. Our relationship was easy. Playing poker, sharing laughs, gathering at the beach with our families. So, you might understand I was still confounded that this road trip involved me visiting James at the Greensville Correctional Center, a medium security prison in south central Virginia. Never having been to a prison before, I began to think about the panic I would experience if confined to a small room for many years. It was unsettling. Can hope exist in an environment of monotony, boredom and inhumane living conditions? Like most free people I took freedom for granted.

As I pulled off the interstate two hours south of Charlottesville, I was stricken with a sick feeling … "I'd forgotten the quarters." There aren't many things you need for a road trip to prison since you are unable to bring along anything other than your automobile key and your license. No wallet, watch, letters or care packages. The one exception is quarters. During your visit vending machines are available for delicious treats such as Funyuns, PayDay candy bars, and Mountain Dew Baja Blast. Compared to prison food, the vending machine goodies provided French Laundry level cuisine. Fortunately, there was a convenience store off the highway in the shadows of the prison. I strode up to the counter with a tenner in my hand only to be told they didn't break change. Frantically I turned the contents of my vehicle upside down and tracked down 15 quarters. I would later learn this was a paltry effort as other visitors had enough quarters to wash and dry a dozen loads of laundry.

I don't know who designs prisons, but if their aim is to intimidate residents and visitors, I'd give them a thumbs up. Set on over 1,000 acres, this facility consists of three unadorned buildings surrounded by guard towers, basketball courts, fencing, and coil upon coil of razor wire. I began walking the perimeter of the parking lot as I arrived 30 minutes early, and even on this day I was determined to get my 10,000 steps recorded on my iWatch. Soon thereafter a prison employee approached in a golf cart to tell me this activity was forbidden and to go back to my car. Resigned, I returned to my vehicle and at 8 A.M. I grabbed my trifling bag of quarters and set upon the visitor's entrance. After registering, I waited for 30 minutes for my name to be called in the first group of visitors. Everything happens slowly at prisons. The corrections officers move methodically and there is a lot of waiting for doors to open. Prison feels weighty and dark. Employees, taught to minimize interaction with inmates, carry a foreboding demeanor.

Sniffing dogs, two full-body pat downs and four different scanners later I found myself locked in an outdoor cage with six other people waiting for the bus to take me to Building 2. Given that there are only three buildings you'd think I had a pretty fair chance of finding Building 2. Wrong. I got off at the second stop which I promptly realized was Building 3. I'm now standing outside of the gate to Building 3 trying to explain to this not terribly understanding CO on an intercom that I'm at the wrong building. I told her that I'd walk the 300 yards to Building 2 and she informed me that this wasn't a good idea. When asked why, she said there'd be a good chance I'd be shot. With that helpful intel I stayed put until the bus corralled me and dropped me off at Building 2. Through two more locked doors and one further pat-down I found myself standing outside the visitor's room of Building 2. At that moment, a pleasantly plump woman turned to me and asked, "Are you here to visit James?"

Caught flat-footed I said, "Yes, how do you know that?" She said all of James's visitors look the same. Not knowing where to go with that I turned toward the door and was ushered through to a table that appeared to be built for a quartet of Oompa Loompas. The table had tiny matching chairs as well. It made me nostalgic for "Romper Room" and the simplicity of childhood. The plain, concrete walled room had about 30 tables and a platform at the front where two corrections officers monitored the goings on between visitors and inmates. Towards the back, there was an alcove that contained four vending machines. So, with my knees brushing up against my chest, I waited for James.

After a few minutes, James ambled in with a huge smile on his face and his prison issued jumpsuit on backwards. I was informed this was to cut down on any sexual shenanigans *sub mensa*. We hugged tightly for 10–15 seconds and settled into our chairs and began catching up. I had a thousand questions for him on life "inside," and he had as many for me on happenings "outside." We talked, laughed, told stories, and fed ourselves with all the delicacies that my 15 quarters could provide. James talked about the Bible study he started and the friends he'd made. He gleefully shared such anecdotes, like how everyone tries to "beat the deuce." Having no clue as to the meaning of this euphemism, he informed me that it was the game of trying to get seconds at each meal without the guards catching you. Personally, he didn't understand the game as he found the food nearly inedible. He said that prison life was, in fact, a lot like how Hollywood has portrayed it over the years. He mentioned how quickly he befriended Carlos, a gay, black man who was the leader of James's pod. Carlos could get you nearly anything you wanted—legal or illegal. It was a side hustle that provided Carlos a steady supply of money and food from the prison canteen. No one crossed Carlos, including even the COs. A few days prior to my visit, James had an altercation with another inmate on the basketball court. Hearing of the incident later that day, Carlos spoke to two guards and by the end of the day James's on court adversary had been transferred to another pod. Just like that. Carlos was also able to get my friend a pillow after James's efforts had fallen on deaf ears for weeks.

As our visit hit the four hour mark I was struck at how quickly the time flew by and most of all how normal it all seemed. We could have just as easily been sitting on his back deck drinking a beer and catching up. I had expected a downtrodden friend too overwhelmed by his circumstances to be present for engaging conversation. His joy, humor, and kindness were not diminished at all by his confinement and his forced separation from his wife and children. There were tender moments as well as he wistfully thought about important moments he'll miss with his family: birthdays, graduations, weddings. A CO ambled over to me and informed me it was time to go. James and I hugged, kissed each other on the cheek, and said goodbye.

I ran the security gauntlet on the way back the same as going in. After twenty minutes or so, I found myself back in my car and assembling my secular armor of watch, keys, cell phone, and wallet and pulling out for the two hour drive north. This road trip turned out far better than I imagined. It also got me thinking of the meaning of freedom. Who was freer? I, with the open road ahead of me, or James, with his confinement? Is freedom measured by wide open spaces or our ability to care for others, be present with the people we love, and adapt to whatever circumstances may be thrown our way? I'm sure James would have traded circumstances with me in a hot minute, but there was much about freedom that I learned in prison that day.

Chris Poe is married to Dianna and has three adult children: Tucker, Emily, and Jake and a grandson, Camden. A long-time resident of Charlottesville, he has been a financial planner for the past 25 years.

TRIP TO MAINE

by Brian McMillen

I WENT ON A ROAD TRIP TO MAINE AFTER MY SECOND YEAR at UVA with my friends Lane and Zach. Lane had been my first-year roommate. He had been a good roommate but we'd become better friends having lived apart. Zach had lived on our hall, too, and had become my best friend in the time since. We didn't have a good reason to visit Maine except that we had some free time and that Zach and Lane both wanted to visit the original L.L.Bean store in Freeport. Our friend Erin had told Zach that she doubted we'd actually commit to a weeklong road trip and that's really what got the three of us all on board.

Zach drove his green Subaru Outback and we would throw out "hang loose" signs with our hands out the window whenever we passed by another "Subey." Lane sat in the passenger's seat and was in control of the aux cable. He played Vampire Weekend, The Shins, Kanye West, and Parachute, and Zach dubbed him "DJ Lazor Lane." I sat in the backseat, read *The Giver*, and slept for most of the drive up. We had left Charlottesville early in the morning and got to New Jersey by lunchtime. I had never been to New Jersey before that point and haven't been after, and all I remember is blacktop and raised highways.

We were staying in Cape Cod at a vacation home that one of Zach's friends had let us use as long as we slept in sleeping bags on the floor of the living room. We planned to spend most of the trip in

Massachusetts and drive up to Maine on one of the days midweek. We got to Cape Cod as it was getting dark and found a bunch of ants in the back of the Subaru as we were unpacking our bags. We ate dinner at the house and then went to the Cape Cod National Seashore. Zach and I liked to smoke Black & Milds, and we smoked on the windy shore while Lane scolded us. Later we rented some movie with Ryan Reynolds from a Redbox and watched it while we did a puzzle.

The next morning we went to a church thrift store and looked for souvenirs. We asked the ladies running the store if there were any sites we should visit and they told us about a lighthouse nearby that we should go check out. We drove to the lighthouse, keeping the same seating arrangement as the day before, and I finished reading *The Giver*. We had with us a stuffed decoy duck named Clint that had become a mascot for our friend group at school. We took some pictures of Clint in front of the lighthouse for posterity, and carried him around to take in the vista, this being his first time visiting the Atlantic Coast. We ended our trip with plenty of pictures of Clint next to all of the important landmarks we visited.

The rest of the week was similarly lackadaisical. We would hear or read about a nearby site to visit and then go to check it out. We spent one afternoon in Provincetown, where we climbed the Pilgrim Monument, ate crab, and browsed through more than a few T-shirts which compared the town's location on the tip of the peninsula to the tip of something else. Another day we went to see Plymouth Rock and then hiked around more of the National Seashore. I have a picture somewhere of Zach on the beach holding up a huge piece of driftwood between his legs.

The day we went up to Maine was really a mixed bag of emotions. There was a satisfaction when we finally pulled up to the L.L.Bean store and got a stranger to take a picture of us with Clint in front of the giant two-story boot outside the store's entrance. But we soon realized that the inventory of the original L.L.Bean store was priced the same as anywhere else and we left to tour the rest of the shopping plaza. I ended up getting a very good sweater at a Goodwill which had a couple lobsters on its side as well as the state's motto: "The way life should be."

I was feeling bad, though, because of a bad case of tonsillitis and Zach has a dietary restriction, so we couldn't find a good place to eat lunch. Eventually, we just gave up on lunch and decided it'd be better to be hungry for our lobster dinner we were planning at a nearby seaside restaurant. The lobster was perfect. But we drove back to Cape Code that night through torrential rain. We kept the same seating arrangement in the car, but we didn't talk or play any music and we went to sleep right when we got home.

We woke up to a new day with nothing to do and I just remember drinking coffee and being happy and proud to have my friends. The drive back to Charlottesville was uneventful, and afterwards we parted ways for the summer. That trip happened right in the middle of my time in college and remains a highlight for me. Zach came over last week and we laughed about how much we don't remember from it.

Brian McMillen is 27 years old. He works as a web developer and lives in Charlottesville, VA with his beautiful wife, Amanda, and his beautiful cat, Boo.

5/3/03

by Jay Varner

DEAR REMO,

That night, after the concert ended, your dad and I sat in the parking lot outside the Bryce Jordan Center and stared in silence at the monolithic steel beams at the base of Beaver Stadium. Back then, staying awake until 2, 3, 4 A.M. meant nothing to us and we were content to wait for the parking lots to empty while chain-smoking cigarettes, recounting setlists, guitar switches, and stage banter. But that night, for the longest time, neither of us could muster up a word.

It was only my second-ever Pearl Jam show, coming just a week after my first in Pittsburgh on April 26, a show I also watched with your dad (who, in between Pittsburgh and State College, watched the April 28 Philly show directly opposite the stage from the last row at the highest level of the old Spectrum). Watching so many shows over such a short period of time wasn't out of the ordinary. Driving three hours to Washington, D.C. or two hours to Baltimore for a show was something we did once or twice a month. We knew concerts but we especially knew Pearl Jam concerts. We had curated a bootleg library that was as admirable in depth as it was alarming in obsession. I say all of this so that when your dad finally tells you his version of May 3, 2003, you don't doubt for a second that what he says is colored by romanticized hindsight. We immediately knew that we'd just witnessed something special, something historic. And we were stunned.

Finally, after who knows how many minutes of silence, he said, "We'll never see another show like that."

"Never," I said.

The cool night air sifted through the open car windows. The last sounds of traffic faded. Leaving this place and this moment would mark the end of something, and endings had been on our minds lately. In eight days, we would graduate from college.

⁂ ⁂ ⁂

Your dad and I grew up in neighboring counties in rural Central Pennsylvania but didn't meet until our first month at college. Those first few weeks were a hard transition for me. My new upper-middle class peers might well have been millionaires. I'd never been around people who drove new cars, lived in nice houses, took actual vacations to different countries. Many had been educated in elite private schools with opportunities I never could never have imagined. They arrived on campus stocked with an analytical, academic lexicon that sounded foreign to my cornpone ears.

The only language I spoke was pop culture. You were born during an era when, thanks to the Internet and capitalism, nerd culture is an accepted and celebrated economic force. However, I grew up in a time when subscribing to *Entertainment Weekly*, counting down the days until the premieres of the latest blockbuster, waiting for an indie gem to show up at the video store, and staying home on Friday nights for *The X-Files* weren't exactly embraced by the mainstream. Yet, those things gave me ballast during four tumultuous years of public high school where any kind of open-mindedness, search for knowledge, or challenging perspective weren't embraced. College would surely deliver some kindred spirits, right?

After my third or fourth international film class and feeling adrift in a sea of pretentious film theory, I blurted out something screenwriter John Ridley had said in an *Entertainment Weekly* interview. It was likely the first time I spoke up in any class beyond answering "here" when roll was called. After class, your dad and I walked back to our dorm together and he mentioned that he'd read that same interview. We started talking about movies, our hometowns, and feeling out of place in college.

How can I even recount the number of things your dad and I did together during those years? The number of movies we watched could program a solid week of cable. The number of concerts we saw is surely one reason for my dulled sense of hearing—as are all the times we turned our guitar amps louder than anybody else would have wanted to hear. We hung out at the radio station on Friday nights, we mailed letters to each over the summer, and we zealously mocked everyone from blockheaded frat guys to pretentious theater majors. We stood numb together on the morning of 9/11 and stared at that clear blue sky, we talked to each other through breakups and crushes, we drank Dunkin Donuts coffee and chain smoked while sitting in a parking lot and listening to new music in his Ford Taurus late into the night.

Music was our constant but Pearl Jam was our cornerstone. We were—and still are—members of the Ten Club, Pearl Jam's official fan club. We learned their songs on guitar, we scoured message boards, we bought magazines, we recorded their performance on *Late Show with David Letterman* and then immediately rewatched. We knew anything that could—legally—be known about the band. But we could never have predicted that the band we'd loved over the course of our friendship would mark the end of our college life by playing in our proverbial backyard.

⁎ ⁎ ⁎

It was a humid Saturday morning with a milky sky, not uncommon for a mid-spring day in Pennsylvania. By the time we drove away from campus, the sun had already begun to burn off the fog. We rolled the windows down, turned up the stereo, and dipped and weaved amongst farm fields and small towns whose best days were far in the past. Fast food restaurants and grocery stores, white churches big and small and as common as mailboxes. Water-logged garage roofs draped by blue tarps, broken windows covered by plywood. A solitary house trailer with front steps of cinder blocks resting at the end of a long and dusty lane. Tireless cars encircled by clusters of rusted household appliances and boxes of machine parts too valuable to throw away, too worthless for much else with. Scrawny dairy cattle stood in muddy pastures dimpled by their hooves. A long climb up the Seven Mountains before that lush, green descent into Happy Valley.

State College housed Penn State University, a land grant university with a powerhouse football team that was the pride of Central Pennsylvania. Both of us grew up watching Nittany Lion football yet felt the 40,000-student campus was simply too massive and overwhelming—a small liberal arts college made sure that we were more than just a number on a roster. But State College had the vibrant, quirky feel of a major college town that pulsed with excitement and life. I would go to State College nearly every weekend during my senior year of high school, watching movies or buying albums and books, daydreaming about my own experience in college. In the end, college was nothing like I'd expected but as perfect as I could have ever hoped.

Maybe we talked about this, though I doubt I would have been emotionally comfortable enough to ever say as much back in those days. And we probably talked a lot about what post-college life would deliver for us. Would we end up back in one of these areas? We were both first-generation college students and I think both of us were a bit unsure about the next step. But, knowing the two of us, we probably just shrugged off the uncertainty, focused on enjoying the day. We stood in line, picked up our fan club tickets and then ate McDonald's. So much of our conversations must have been ordinary, that shared language of friends.

And the concert? Look, I could totally geek out here and overwhelm you with every single beat of this show. I could write thousands of words describing the minutiae of this show. But your dad has the live album and I think you need to discover those things with a fresh set of ears. But let me tell you three things.

First, I remember talking to your dad during the first encore break that we sense some kind of magical energy was percolating. The band started extending some songs—"rearviewmirror" and "Daughter" are both nearly nine minutes—and looked to be genuinely excited to be playing together.

After the second encore break, Eddie Vedder walked back on stage and said, "If you're willing to stick around, we'll make this the longest Pearl Jam show we've ever played." Now, Ed is an accomplished, skillful frontman—in the right moment, he truly can make you believe that you're part of the best audience the band has ever seen. So, at first, we took that statement with a grain of salt. But that second encore just kept going. There's an art to a good setlist, and this was the band in peak form. Each song built upon the last, raising the energy in that room. It was like a series of climaxes—whether it be all-out rocking versions of songs or dusting off some deep cuts that they hadn't played in years—this show just kept going.

After that third encore break, the band reemerged on stage and Ed said, "At this point, we're daring you to leave." And then I heard the A-minor strum that opened the cover of Victoria Williams' "Crazy Mary." This song remains the single-best concert experience I've witnessed, a band fully alive and meshing together to create something I've listened to at least once a month since that night. Ed nailed his most memorable lines—"No L-O-I-T-E-R-I-N-G A-llowed" and "Take a bottle, drink it down, pass it around"—and hit his soaring cries at the end of the verses before bowing out as the mighty Boom Gasper, the newest addition to the band, turned his B3 and Leslie into a whirring and swirling tornado, feeding into a Mike McCready guitar solo that so seared across his Stratocaster's frets that I imagine some smoke still hovers atop the venue. Even the usually reserved Stone Gossard got into the moment, strumming his Taylor acoustic so hard that I can't imagine how he didn't rip the strings out of their pegs. When I listen to it today, it's clear that drummer Matt Cameron tries to lead the band into a rousing crescendo on the song. But they just kept going.

For three hours and ten minutes, they just kept going.

* * *

Your dad turned the key on the ignition and fired up the engine in the Taurus that had carried us so many miles over the years. We drove along the Pennsylvania highways and backroads we knew as well as the live Pearl Jam songs we played on the stereo until we arrived at the campus that we'd soon bid farewell.

Who knows how many miles we've each traveled since then? I've moved—to North Carolina and finally to Charlottesville, Virginia—but through it all your dad and I have remained close, probably not going more than a week without talking to each other in some way. And there have been many more PJ shows together—in Asheville, North Carolina, in Washington, D.C., in Philly. And there have been many more PJ shows apart and with our wives. Each time, whether together or apart, we talk about the setlists, the guitars, the differences we see as the band members settle into their mid-fifties. Every show, of course, has been special, but none have compared to State College. At least, not yet.

March of 2020 was supposed to have been your first PJ show. Of course, the pandemic forced all of us to make new plans. You'll have to wait a bit longer but maybe that will be the concert that tops State College. You already know the music; your dad has played them for you not long after you were born.

And someday, you will have a band that you love so much it hurts. Perhaps it will be Pearl Jam, perhaps not. Whatever that band, may they deliver you as much joy and comfort and excitement as I've felt. And may you get to share all of it with your best friend.

Jay Varner, 39, is a Lecturer in the School of Writing, Rhetoric, and Technical Communication at James Madison University. He's previously taught in the MFA program at Hollins University, at Piedmont Virginia Community College, and at the University of Virginia. His memoir, *Nothing Left to Burn*, was published by Algonquin Books and his work has appeared in *BOMB*, *The Black Warrior Review*, *Oxford American Magazine*, and numerous other places.

SPRING BREAK BASEBALL PILGRIMAGE

by Sam Carr

ALL BALLPLAYERS THINK ABOUT THEIR MUSIC. "WALK up" to the plate music for their at bats. Warm up music and batting practice music. Music to play in the locker room after practice on Fridays, after trips to the training room to ice shoulders and elbows. And then there is the music that 16- to 18-year-old players listen to in the van on the spring break team trip to Florida.

The Florida spring break trip is a ritualistic pilgrimage for ballplayers early in the school ball season. Then, like migrating flocks of birds, teams return gelled and ready for their conference rivals before splintering into even more tribes for summer teams.

It wasn't my first trip to Florida to play ball, but I had transferred schools and was the "new guy" from the Sun Belt, and this would be my first trip with this established team and a new coach. He is known as "Coach" in high school. Not "chief" or "skipper" or even "Mr. [Teacher's name]"—he is all of that and more: a cerebral, educated disciplinarian who can invoke "in loco parentis" and run you under the sun until you throw up your motel continental breakfast or launch missiles at you with his fungo bat. Though only in his late thirties, he seemed fifty and was in military lingo "the Old Man." He checked your rooms at 10 P.M. and required polished spikes before games. Since this was my first trip with the squad, I had a lot to prove on these Florida diamonds—at morning practices and afternoon or night games. Not just to earn a place in the lineup, but I needed to prove myself as one of the team.

As we journeyed from highway truck-stop motels to high school fields, my teammates astutely sized up the dynamic of the three vans rented by our head coach and the two assistants. The seniors and the wily juniors sprung for the vans driven by the relatively fun assistant coaches. Other juniors like myself who were polite and slow were left to fill the empty seats in Coach's van. Just like the lack of social mobility at the school lunch tables, once you were seated in a van on the road trip it was for the long haul.

From when we first took infield warm-ups before the first game and as the campaign wore on, I established my mettle in the field. I showcased my best impression of Pete Rose or Kenny Lofton on the base paths. I even proved I could platoon the outfield. On and off the field, I was breaking in. I still didn't fully participate in the motel and dugout antics, but I looked on and chuckled. But in the van, even on the last full day of playing ball on the trip, I was still pretty quiet.

"Guys, how about the radio?" Coach said to the worn players in the back. Somewhere in the middle of the orange groves, we won the first of two games of the day in dramatic come-from-behind fashion. I was so dirty from diving back into first base to avoid the pitcher's several pick off attempts it was like I was dancing the gator in the dirt. Slinking into the middle row, I nursed a sweaty Gatorade. I could feel my muscles tighten in the air conditioning. But our work wasn't done for the day. We victors departed for Okeechobee, and without taking requests Coach dialed in the classic rock station. Guitar riffs herald the first chords of Whitesnake's "Here I Go Again" as we all reverently listened and let the music stir us.

No I don't know where I am going.
But I sure know where I've been.
Hanging on the promises in songs of yesterday
And I've made up my mind
I ain't wasting no more time.

Though I keep searching for an answer.
I never seem to find what I'm look for.
Oh Lord I pray you give me strength to carry on ...

(Chorus) *Here I go again on my own.*
Going down the only road I've ever known.

The Gatorade and adrenaline kicked in, and butterflies before yet another game disappeared. We had work to do, and we all felt it. No one spoke as we all nodded along to the song.

But, here I go again
Here I go again
Here I go again
Here I GOOOOOOOOO

After a few more songs on the typical Florida classic rock station, Coach decided he had reminisced over the music of his era enough and relinquished control of the stereo.

"Let's listen to something else. Sammy, what music did you bring?" Coach said, knowing well that we teenage guys of the circa 2000 era all downloaded copyright-infringed songs and burned mix CDs for all occasions.

"Umm. Umm. Yes, coach. I have got a few things here," I mumbled.

I—less of the new guy I was days earlier but still new—was ambushed: I felt as if I were called to do math on the blackboard in front of the class, and didn't know which mix CD to grab. Here was my turn. None of my mixes had organization or progression. It was a shotgun blast of a playlist, a collage of my MP3 collection that only had meaning to me. Here was my judgment before the whole van, not my batting average or defensive stops: whether my playlist would sufficiently connect with and motivate our van. I chose a burned CD from its sleeve and waited as each song played like a chef waiting for his diners to finish their courses. George Strait and Billy Idol.

Rick Springfield? *Strike 3!* I thought. *Walk back to the dugout.*

In my mind the CD played for hours. Each bar was a lifetime. When the playlist concluded, Coach looked into the rearview mirror and said with a grin, "Sammy, what—no 'Blue Suede Shoes' and Johnny Cash?? I'm kidding. That was good. Thanks."

The rest of the guys nodded. I passed.

Sam Carr, 35, is a small businessman, outdoorsman, and sports enthusiast. When he's not driving, then he's probably reading.

GOIN' TO CAROLINA

by Michael Kuchinski

IT WAS THE SUMMER OF 2006. OUR FAMILY VACATION WAS approaching and, as was our custom, we were planning to go to North Carolina's Crystal Coast. Having gone there every summer since the children were little, the trip generally involved bucketing down the interstate for six hours. Invariably, we would arrive at our destination hot, tired, and cranky.

My son Will, then a rising junior at Davidson College, had different ideas. He proposed a more leisurely, laid back journey, spread out over a couple of days. His plan was that we would drive down the coast, avoiding roads that had more than two lanes. We would stop at points of interest along the way, spend a night on Ocracoke Island, and motor on to our final destination the next day.

The idea intrigued me. I have always been fascinated by accounts of road trips, from Kerouac's *On the Road* to Steinbeck's *Travels with Charley*. And while this two-day journey was far less epic than either of these, we could still lay claim to membership in the road tripper's pantheon.

As usual, we planned to take two cars. Traveling light is not a concept our family has ever been able to embrace. The trunks and back seats of both vehicles would be laden not just with luggage, but food, beverages, beach umbrellas, inflatable rafts, and camp chairs. With Will as the navigator, he and I would be in the lead car. My wife Alison, our friend Caroline, and Will's twin sister Layton, would follow behind.

And so we left our house in Fredericksburg early one morning, and headed down Route 17. I knew this leg of the journey fairly well. Working for the Department of the Navy at the time, this was my preferred route to reach the sprawling Naval Station at Norfolk. It took us through a part of Virginia seldom seen. Just south of Norfolk, we crossed into North Carolina. There, we picked up Route 158, skirted Currituck Sound, and crossed the Wright Memorial Bridge. We were now officially in the Outer Banks.

Our first stop was Kitty Hawk, at the Wright Brothers' Museum and Monument. Only a replica of Orville and Wilbur's fabled prototype, the *Wright Flyer*, is displayed there. The original resides at the Smithsonian's Air and Space Museum.

From there we followed Route 12, down the barrier islands, past Kill Devil Hills, and Nag's Head, until we came to Bodie Island Lighthouse. Lighthouses figured prominently on our trip. Each one was a photo opportunity and necessitated a stop.

We crossed onto Pea Island, a designated bird sanctuary and wildlife refuge. Most of the land was undeveloped. There were miles and miles of sand dunes and scrub pines, and little else. The utility poles that lined the road were the only hint of civilization.

Will was eager to get to Chicamacomico, site of the country's first life-saving station, established in 1874. He had researched it thoroughly. But when we got there, it was closed. We stopped briefly, and peered through the darkened windows, but there wasn't another soul around. Disappointed, we moved on.

Our next stop brought us to the Cape Hatteras Lighthouse, where Will, Caroline, and I mounted the 287 steps to reach the observation platform. We were rewarded for our efforts with a magnificent view of the ocean and the neighboring beaches.

From Hatteras, it was a forty minute ferry ride to Ocracoke Island. Landing at the north end, we drove through still more barren sand dunes and scrub pines, until finally we came to Ocracoke Village. We took up residence at Blackbeard's Lodge, a friendly if somewhat eccentric, pirate-themed establishment where we were booked for the night. It turned out the proprietor knew Alison and Caroline. She had once worked at the same library where they worked.

We had a nice dinner at a restaurant called The Back Porch, which was right across the street from the lodge. I don't know if Ocracoke has any night life, but we didn't stay up to find out. We were tired from the day's journey and wanted to get an early start the next day.

We awoke to thunderstorms and rain. Good weather for ducks, as the old joke goes, and there were plenty of them, waddling through the streets, seemingly unperturbed by the presence of us humans. After a big breakfast, we took a driving tour around this offbeat little island community, which included an obligatory stop at Ocracoke Lighthouse.

We happened upon a British Cemetery, maintained by the Ocracoke Coast Guard Station. There, we found a memorial to the crew of *HMS Bedfordshire*, an armed trawler. She was sunk off the coast by a German U-boat, May 11, 1942. All hands were lost. The men whose bodies were recovered are interred at the cemetery.

Before noon, the rain stopped, and we queued up for the ferry that would take us to Cedar Island. The ferry ride took over two hours, but we had brought along bag lunches, and passed the time eating, reading, and napping. A man in a NC State cap spotted my Davidson T-shirt, and we struck up a conversation.

Our car was one of the first to disembark, but the ladies, stuck behind a lumbering motor home during the ferry ride, weren't so lucky. Will and I went on ahead, as we needed to get to our destination before the rental agency closed.

By some reckoning, Ocracoke marks the end of the Outer Banks, but the scenery was little changed. We drove through more desolate countryside, the road a ribbon between salt marshes. Occasionally, there would be clusters of houses, signifying some little town or hamlet, but mostly it was wilderness.

In due course, the landscape became less isolated, and more populous. Traffic picked up. We came to places whose names we recognized, and we knew that our journey was coming to an end.

First, there was Beaufort and right after that Moorehead City. We crossed the Atlantic Beach Bridge to Bogue Banks, and all the little communities along that barrier island. We drove through Pine Knoll Shores, Salter Path, and finally Emerald Isle, our destination. Will and I picked up the keys to the beach house, anticipating a week of rest and relaxation, and reveling in the satisfaction of having chosen the road less traveled.

Michael Kuchinski is 67 years old and an instructor in the Mathematics Department at Germanna Community College.

TWO JOURNEYS HOME

by Robbie Sapunarich

ON THE MORNING OF MONDAY, AUGUST 5TH, 2019, I left my home of 18 years to make the long drive home.

Jenoa and I woke dark and early on air mattresses at my parents' house. We dressed and washed and gathered the few belongings we had with us. We said goodbye to my parents. We drove to our apartment through the empty early-morning streets of the Orange County, California, suburb where I had lived since I was eleven. The air was dry, calm, and temperate, the sun's absence giving a brief reprieve from the scorching, arid days. We pulled into the parking lot of our apartment complex, the darkness punctuated by the harsh orange lights shining on the carports and walkways. We walked up the stairs of our stucco building and entered our apartment, where Jones, our cat, greeted us with an anxious and irritated meow. Our cat, her litter box, and her food and water bowls were all that remained in the space that a few weeks ago was filled with our possessions. We put Jones in her crate and brought her to the Prius downstairs. I locked the door of the place that we called home for the past two years of our marriage. I put the key under the doormat for the landlord. I walked down the stairs, hopped in the passenger seat of the car, and we left.

⁕ ⁕ ⁕

It seems to me now that much of my adult life so far has been an ongoing series of road trips. Not always in the hit-the-road-with-your-buddies-in-search-of-adventure sense—although that has been part of it—but in the sense that much of my life has been spent behind the wheel or in the passenger seat of a car. Southern California is known for being a car culture; its wide freeways and (sub)urban sprawl are almost impossible to navigate without a car. Walkable neighborhoods are a rare treat. And it's not uncommon to have your day spread across multiple cities and municipalities, working in one, shopping for groceries in another, visiting friends in a third, and finally coming home to park your car in yet another, and this not counting the cities that you might drive through to get from one to another. A friend once remarked to me that the quickest it will take you to get almost anywhere in south Orange County is fifteen minutes. I commuted forty-five minutes three days a week to my job in Huntington Beach (mercifully, I worked from home twice a week). My father often spent his days commuting two hours each way to and from his office in Torrance for over ten years.

Southern California's mobile culture affected more than the quotidian acts of commuting and errand-running though. When I reflect on my teens and early to mid twenties, so much of my recreation involved adventures on the road—trips to LA and San Diego to visit breweries, attend concerts, and shop at record stores; giving my friend in the Army a lift to Fort Irwin out in the Mojave Desert, followed by a three and a half hour drive to meet up with my parents in San Diego; longer trips along the length of California.

The landscape of these journeys always filled me with a sense of intrepid wonder. Wandering beyond south Orange County meant leaving the placid sights of manicured greenbelts, cookie cutter homes, and planned communities. To the east, along Interstate 15, the Mojave Desert spread out, while to the north was LA, with its endless sea of urban sprawl, and beyond that, the Grapevine and the Central Valley. Leaving Orange and Los Angeles counties was a move from density to desolation—the miles of concrete and stucco gave way to open, arid spaces. I felt a sense of being unmoored, adrift, disoriented, but the surreality of the journey was always tempered by the surety of returning home.

⁂ ⁂ ⁂

The early morning darkness faded to purple and orange as we drove east into the sunrise. We made our way to Interstate 10, driving through Riverside and Palm Springs, where we had vacationed only a month before. Jones intermittently let out a deep and whiny meow from her crate in the backseat. We eventually made it to the Arizona border, driving deeper and deeper into the desert territory that we were ultimately leaving. Jenoa's always liked the desert, and while I find something enchanting about it, it's also always instilled a sort of anxiety in me that I find hard to describe. Maybe it's the lack of water or greenery, but whenever I'm in it I'm filled with the sense that I am not meant to be there. To me, it is territory to sojourn, never settle.

Jenoa and I had ventured beyond the comfortable confines of the coastal counties a few times in the year preceding our move. A day trip to Tijuana, a weekend in Las Vegas, and a proper do-nothing vacation in Palm Springs were a few highlights of the months before we left the west. Two of those adventures, Vegas and Palm Springs, required driving east, like we were now. But this time, we wouldn't be driving back on the westbound freeway. As we drove deeper into the deserts of Arizona and New Mexico, where we would spend our first night on the trip, the reality of the previous day's goodbyes settled in more and more. Home was behind us as much as it was ahead.

⁂ ⁂ ⁂

Jenoa was living in Oakland when we first met, so the earliest days of our relationship were characterized by great distances. We both made a few trips from from southern to northern California, and vice versa, during that time. We also made trips out of California together. Some of these were to visit her family in Texas. Another one was to visit my extended family in the tri-state area, and attend the Mockingbird conference in New York City (a conference which, through the friends we made there, would arguably be responsible for our new journey to Charlottesville). But the last trip of the long-distance phase of our relationship would be the day she left Oakland to move to Orange County and be with me.

The morning of that trip, I woke early, and my father gave me a ride from my childhood home to Long Beach Airport to take the day's first flight to Oakland. I can't recall anything from that flight. I landed in Oakland sometime around eight in the morning. Jenoa picked me up, and we ate breakfast at a now-defunct diner that was owned by one of the members of Green Day. We drove to her apartment and packed her belongings into her car, and left Oakland before noon. The overcast skies of the Bay Area yielded to the hot, sunny air of the Central Valley. We drove through the now-familiar landscape of orchards and farms and ranches, occasionally interrupted by gas stations and rest stops. The agricultural landscape was set amid vast seas of brown grass. An interminable power line off the east side of the ride stretched into the distance. Interstate 5 eventually took us to mountains of the Grapevine, where the Central Valley ends and what my perception recognizes as Southern California begins. We drove through Los Angeles and into Orange County. We ate burritos and mussels at Bear Flag Fish Company in Newport Coast, a ritzy area on bluffs that overlook the Pacific. We finally arrived my house, where a sign reading "For Sale" had been put up that day, sometime between my early morning departure and our return.

I knew that my parents were planning to sell their house, since my dad would be retiring soon, and their retirement plans included moving out of California. Still, that knowledge didn't change the fact that on this return to home, the feelings of groundedness and stability that had been dependably present after previous trips never returned, and the sense of being unmoored and adrift remained. In a few weeks after our return I moved out of my parents' home, as did Jenoa. About three months after that we were engaged, and five months after our engagement we married. After that we went on countless journeys, and always returned home, but for the both of us, the sense that we were home returned less and less.

* * *

We eventually arrived in Cloudcroft, New Mexico, where we spent our first night. The following day, we drove down the mountain to the eastern part of New Mexico, with its vast spaces that rivaled the openness of anything I remembered in California. The flat, dry landscapes of New Mexico and west Texas gave way to the Hill Country, before finally bringing us to Jenoa's childhood home in Glen Rose, where we spent two nights with her parents. On our interim day there we went swimming in the Paluxy River at Dinosaur State Park, where one can still find fossilized dinosaur steps in the riverbed. We left our cat with Jenoa's parents, since our new apartment wouldn't allow pets. On Thursday we drove through Arkansas and Tennessee, where we stayed with my boss at his home near Nashville. Friday we drove the final stretch of our journey along Interstate 81, through the Blue Ridge Mountains, and into Charlottesville.

We moved into the temporary lodgings of a furnished apartment with the few belongings we had brought with us, and made a frantic trip to CVS when we realized that we didn't own any soap, or toilet paper, or shampoo. The following Monday, three days after arriving in Charlottesville, I took a flight for a business trip back to Southern California, to the place I had previously called home.

Over the last five months of 2019, I would make five more trips by air out of our new home, either with Jenoa or by myself. Three of those trips were back to California. By December, the sense of being adrift had reached a saturation point. But upon each return, I felt a little more at home. I took a new job that was based in Charlottesville, and I decided to minimize work travel in 2020.

Of course, minimizing travel became an involuntary decision in 2020. We had planned to visit Britain to walk along St. Cuthbert's Way, fly to California to visit friends in July, and make a couple of trips to Texas to visit Jenoa's family. Instead, for the time being, we are grounded at home.

But I'm grateful to be grounded in the place we are. As much as I miss Southern California and the friends I have there, the people and place that now characterize our daily life have been a Godsend. Sometimes I hear complaints about traffic and the lack of public transportation in Charlottesville, and while they have their merits, the backlog of podcasts that I used to listen to for sanity in Orange County traffic speaks to how much less time I spend in a car. The dying and blooming of deciduous trees and the passing of seasons marks time in a more palpable way than did the chaparral landscapes I was accustomed to for most of my life. Fortuitous run-ins with friends and acquaintances while walking downtown or at a park are a common occurrence, even in the midst of a pandemic that requires us to be momentarily isolated. Although I'm anxious and ready to set foot on the road and venture somewhere again, I'm more than thankful, right now, to be home.

Robbie Sapunarich is a writer and software developer in Charlottesville, Virginia, where he lives with his wife, Jenoa, and their cat, Jones. He blogs at robertsapunarich.com.

TRAVELOGUE

by Kathy Zentgraf

NORMALLY, OUR TRIPS LOOKED SOMETHING LIKE THIS: we piled too many bags, blankets, pillows, people into our most reliable Volvo wagon. Though at one point, a beige Jeep Wagoneer with fake wood sides took us to Maine and back. I'm not a fan of suitcases so there were always a number of baskets with food, towels, clothes, my best knife—whatever I thought we'd need for our vacation once we got where we were going. A series of coolers were tucked at our feet with the largest one in the way back. I don't believe in fast food except Dairy Queen so we stopped to eat when I had picked out a town with a decent grocery store and a high school with an outdoor track. A little bit of trial and error went into this process as I was choosing towns from a map, based on how big and dark the name of the town was written on my Rand McNally. We weren't going to stop in a town with the spidery font of say, Junction, West Virginia, but we might try the bolder print Sweet Springs. This theory had holes in it—you can miss some unforgettable places like Elkins, West Virginia, by basing your decision on font. To say that some divination was involved in picking the right town is irritating to anyone who is a spreadsheet guy. My husband wanted the first pick to be the right one which I sadly could never promise. The ensuing madness pleased me, irritated him, added hours to the trip. But there you go—marriage! family! road trip!

Most decent sized high schools have tracks around their football fields, so once I picked a town we cruised the school grounds to make sure we could get in. Sometimes I'd drop my husband and the kids there to run around while I shopped, other times we all went to the store. Either way, we'd end up back there, unpacking coolers, adding food from the store—running, walking, skipping, many competitions begun and ended, some singing, some fighting. We stopped rain or shine—our kids saying at first how stupid it was, they weren't getting out of the car this time, it was too hot/cold/wet. Until it caught on. I don't know when it did or how. Maybe in the grocery when they saw that I'd cave on food choices. No nacho cheese Doritos, but yeah, we need the big peanut M&M's.

My husband and I continued this tradition—even when we were pressed to get back to work on a Sunday afternoon from our girls' college 12 hours from home. Our go-to town for the first stop: Wooster, Ohio. After four and a half hours in the car, we cheated by ordering sandwiches and then going to the high school. We added a nap under a shade tree. When I look back, I think it's still the best way to travel long distances with a carload of toddlers, middle schoolers, cooler than cool high school students. Maybe this tipped the scales—by the time they were eight or nine, I, their English teacher mother, required an essay from each of them if they fought in the car.

So, wasn't that track enticing?

Kathy Zentgraf lives in Charlottesville with her husband, Tony. She likes to think, write, teach, and cook.

"WHERE HAVE YOU GONE, JOE DIMAGGIO?"

by Jim Barns

IN THE WINTER OF 1968 I HITCHHIKED FROM STOCKTON, California, to New York City, 69 rides in six weeks. A memorable episode came in Texas. I was headed to New Orleans for Mardi Gras when a guy in a convertible, top down, picked me up. A very talkative, friendly guy. Right away he talked about a movie he'd seen the night before, *The Graduate*. "You have to see it," he exclaimed.

I arrived in New Orleans after dark. Walking down Canal Street, I saw a movie marquee: *The Graduate*. I thought, "What the heck ..." It is the only time I have sat through a movie twice. I certainly related to Benjamin, Dustin Hoffman's character, but watching the film years later it did not add up. When back in school at Williams, I went to an informal talk by alum and author of *The Graduate*, Charles Webb. He certainly fit the personality of Benjamin in the book! A bit befuddled.

For a decade after college, Jim Barns was a rambler. He settled down in Charlottesville as a reference librarian for 29 years at the public library. Recently, someone commented that he thought of Jim as the "Mr. Rogers" of the library.

NEVER GET BACK

by Cortlandt Schoonover

"Oh, somewhere in this favoured land the sun is shining bright;
the band is playing somewhere, and somewhere hearts are light ..."
—**Phin**

THERE WAS A HALF-BAKED PITCH TO THE *OXFORD American.* I think Josh wrote it. He ended up sending it within a month of our proposed departure date, so that's why you're reading this recap seven years later in a road trip anthology, rather than in the big-leagues of *OA*'s Summer 2013 issue. There were four of us that actually traveled on the trip. Josh was a baker and a recently retired high school teacher. Ray had given up a job in consulting to go work for the school board that oversaw most of New Orleans's public schools. Nic and I were musicians, which meant that we didn't make any money. Together, we had a shared love of baseball, and a crazy plan to see 10 minor league games in 10 days. We did end up publishing our own blog at the time, but I think the only readers were our moms and my baseball-loving uncle.

The Southern League is made up of ten teams. It's bounded by Jackson, Mississippi, to Jacksonville, Florida, east to west, and from Kodak, Tennessee, to Mobile, Alabama, north to south. It's a Double-A league. Out of our traveling party of four, I remain the least knowledgeable about baseball. I believe Double-A was exciting to us because Major League teams often let their top young prospects play at that level, and skip right over Triple-A into the Major Leagues when the teams deem the player ready. So although the quality of play may be higher in Triple-A, the caliber of prospects in Double-A outclasses them. Plus we lived in New Orleans, and this road trip seemed cooler than figuring out how to get to Albuquerque. (The Isotopes play in the same league as the Zephyrs.) Plus, who could pass up a chance to visit all these small to mid-sized Southern cities?

We had a plan. Josh and I were making the whole trip of ten cities in ten days. Ray would join us for the first five games, then bus back to New Orleans and start his new job the next day. Nic would then arrive via train to Birmingham and join us for the latter five dates. Our friend and roommate, Michael, could not come, but in his infinite kindness he lent us his Honda Civic in exchange for two oil changes. (Often minor league teams give away oil changes as a promotion to those sitting in a lucky seat. We never won an oil change.) I was in charge of coffee for the trip, so I opted to outfit the car with an inverter to plug in a percolator. We accidentally shattered the carafe within an hour of being on the road. Morale was low.

Night one was the Huntsville Stars. The home team got clobbered by the Jackson (TN) Generals, 8–3. We had forgettable burgers in a forgettable strip mall, but had the pleasure of staying in a Hampton Inn that Ray paid for with his hotel points. Ray had accumulated a lot of Hampton Inn points over the course of business travel, and he was generous enough to share what he could with the group over the course of the trip. That covered our lodging for some but not all of the nights.

Day two was where things picked up. We only had a quick two-hour drive to see the Chattanooga Lookouts host the Mobile BayBears. The Lookouts had a great stadium and at the time big-time prospect Yasiel Puig played for the team. He had defected from Cuba, and to be honest, looked bored to have to waste his time playing in Double-A. He was easily more athletic and just plain more talented than anyone else on the field.

During the course of the close game, we made friends with a couple of women our age sitting next to us. After a bit of chit-chat about the game, we noticed that one of them kept looking at her iPhone, at an app called Tinder, which we had heard of, but never had used before. We asked her about it. It was a dating app. You could see profiles of strangers nearby, and swipe right on the touchscreen of your phone to indicate interest. If they were interested as well, you could begin flirting. She was currently chatting with one of the starting pitchers for the Lookouts (he wasn't pitching that game). We were mesmerized. She showed us the somewhat dull conversation she and the pitcher were having. I guess I'd be lying if I said I was totally mentally engaged during every baseball game I watch as a fan. (Zoning out is one of the joys of baseball spectatorship, in particular.) But this player was just straight up ignoring the game and focusing on the afterparty! I guess off days are the benefit of pitching.

We ended up driving up Lookout Mountain with the ladies, after having had several beers at a bar downtown. They say you can see seven states from Lookout Mountain, but the suds had my head spinning. Any details of the Civil War battle gleaned off of historical plaques remain fuzzy. Our new friends wanted to link up with the Lookouts' pitcher, but we had to meet Jonathan, our friend and host.

The next day brought a scrappy game of two-on-two basketball at the Chattanooga YMCA, and a quick drive for a day game hosted by the Tennessee Smokies in Kodak. The visiting Birmingham Barons prevailed 9–7, as either the bats were hot, or the pitchers weren't hot prospects. I mostly remember the haunting calls of Woody Woodpecker as played over the PA system after the visiting team made an error. (And terrifyingly mimicked by the thousands of Cub Scouts in attendance.)

We had no place to stay in Kodak. Our hotel points had to be rationed for the many nights remaining. We came up with a plan. Savannah, Georgia, was only a six-hour drive away, and coincidentally was hosting a Sand Gnats game that evening (For completeness's sake, the Sand Gnats are Single-A, and therefore not an official part of our long strange tour). If we left right away, we could catch some of that game and see Savannah's stadium, which was rumored to have hosted Babe Ruth and Lou Gehrig in 1926, the year it was built. As for lodging, Josh made a Craigslist post entitled "Three Gentlemen in Savannah." For those unaware, the most savory transaction one makes on Craigslist is something like giving away furniture with some sort of insect infestation. Josh's post felt dangerous. But maybe it was dangerous in a good way. Regardless, we needed a backup plan, so we decided that we would download Tinder, try to get some matches, and then explain we weren't looking for any romance, just a floor or couch for a few baseball-loving guys to sleep on. I was the sacrificial lamb who had to make an actual Tinder profile for the experiment.

The drive to Savannah took a bit longer than we thought. We got to the ballpark in the bottom of the ninth and the Sand Gnats' gate attendant let us in to the game for free. The stadium was historical, small, and everyone was walking out of it because the game was over. We went downtown to grab some beers and lick our wounds. We found a place that we believed to be near Savannah College of Art and Design, a place called The Alley Cat. I'm not even going to fact-check that, so anyone who is familiar with Savannah, feel free to laugh at me if I'm wrong. We drank a few beers. We weren't getting a lot of matches on Tinder. No one replied to our Craigslist post. We approached a group of people at the bar and explained our predicament. They weren't too entertained, and didn't seem to be enticed by our offer. To be fair, our offer was for us, three complete strangers, to sleep on any available surface. One girl called us "bandos," which was possibly an insult, and was at least a term with which I was unfamiliar. Our next attempt had promise. We made friends with a really funny SCAD student. She had a great living room where we could stay; it even had two couches. She just had to check with her boyfriend, who was arriving at the bar any minute, but she was sure he'd say yes. Time slipped away from us in the way sometimes does in bars, and the boyfriend arrived around closing time. He was a minor league baseball player. (Single-A Short Season, but still!) But as we stumbled out into the night, he had second thoughts on hosting us as houseguests, and we said our goodbyes. We had no place to stay, so we drove to Tybee Island and slept a fitful few hours on the beach.

We drove to Jacksonville. It was Dale Murphy meet-and-greet night. I think we decided that the line was too long, or maybe we were too tired. Sorry all you Dale Murphy fans. We went to go stay at Josh's friend's house. She was a dolphin trainer, which I imagine is a pretty common job for a Floridian. Somehow the communication got mixed up, and she thought it was only Josh staying, or maybe she thought we would smell less like we had slept on a beach the previous night. Also her in-laws were there, helping her and her husband move into their new home. Ray and I talked for a bit to her father-in-law about dolphins, while Josh tried to sort things out, but in the end, we decided we'd drive onward to Montgomery that night. We made it to the middle-of-nowhere Georgia before Ray dipped into the stash of hotel points. I've never been more thankful for a Hampton Inn.

I actually skipped the game in Montgomery. I'm a bit sad about that. It was extra-innings, and they have the best team name: the Montgomery Biscuits. Their mascot is a biscuit with a little pat of butter on him. I was busing back to New Orleans to host the punk-rock band Titus Andronicus at our somewhat empty house. Then I'd take the train with Nic to meet back up with Josh. Somehow Titus Andronicus changed their show time, so I missed the actual show. I found this out via text message five minutes after the bus back home left the strip-mall parking lot. It was a lonely, sad bus ride. I tried texting with the band's manager to say how sad I was, but all I got out of it was an increasing number of friends on the guest list.

But I did get to see Titus Andronicus do karaoke at Kajun's Pub afterward. I talked some baseball with them as well. They were all big Mets fans, if I'm not mistaken. I had to leave early in the morning, and Michael (remember how he lent us his car) made them smoothies for breakfast and washed the dishes after them at the house. He rated them five out of ten as houseguests, which I think is generous. But Michael is a generous guy.

Nic and I took the train up to Birmingham. Josh met us at the station. He had slept in the car. He was awakened by a neighborhood security patrol halfway through the night and had to find a new place to park and sleep. It sounded stressful. When famous sneaker salesman Michael Jordan retired from basketball, he spent a few years playing for the Birmingham Barons. They had a fancy new stadium. We were tired. We left the game before it was over. Good People Brewery is right across the street. Somehow the owner found out we could play music. (I think Nic told him; Josh would never admit to that.) He told us to get our instruments from the car, and we played a short and quiet set in the courtyard. He gave us free beer and 20 bucks, which is honestly one of the more financially successful gigs that I've ever had. We got some barbecue at a restaurant. We were thinking hard about how we had no place to stay, so we went back to the brewery. A guy stopped us and asked if we were the musicians from earlier. We said yes, and he and his roommates let us stay on their couches and bought us pizza. Only halfway through the trip, I'll leave you with that image of the kindness of strangers, and a promise that I'll tell you about the rest of the trip sometime if you let me stay on your couch.

Cortlandt Schoonover lives in New Orleans, Louisiana. During more than a decade of writing shorts, he has been published in the zines *Neutrons/ Protons* and *Compound Sentences*. In his spare time, Cortlandt develops software for the Louisiana Department of Health. He enjoys baking bread, playing soccer, and playing video and/or board games with friends.

BLUES, BLUEGRASS, AND BARBECUE

by Proal Heartwell

"LADIES AND GENTLEMEN, I'VE JUST RECEIVED SOME sad news: B.B. King has passed away," announces Daddy Rich from the stage of the Ground Zero Blues Club in Clarksdale, Mississippi, on July 7, 2009. A chorus of disbelief erupts from the blues aficionados patronizing the club, just a stone's throw from the "Crossroads," the intersection of Highways 61 and 49 where Robert Johnson sold his soul to the devil. My wife, Susie; my daughter, Elise; and I are among these patrons, and like the others in attendance, we mourn the death of the great bluesman from Itta Bena, Mississippi. But there is only one problem: Daddy Rich is misinformed, and after a few minutes, during which the bar does a brisk business, a club manager takes the stage and announces that the King of the Blues is alive and well. (In fact, B.B. King lives another six years, dying in 2015 at age 89.) Daddy Rich, a native of Clarksdale, mumbles an apology, shrugs his shoulders, and continues his set. And despite his blistering guitar work and howling vocals, his performance is somehow diminished in my mind after his misguided proclamation. However, the evening is not lost, because soon the incomparable Super Chikan takes the stage with his homemade electric shotgun guitar, and his playing frenzies the crowd like a rattlesnake handling evangelist.

It has been a long day, the fourth of our self-designated "Blues, Bluegrass, and Barbecue" tour. That morning finds us in Memphis where we have tickets for the day's first tour of Graceland. With our headsets secure, we are shepherded through Elvis's home with disciples from around the world, each listening to the recorded information in his or her native tongue. (How do you say, "You ain't nothin' but a hound dog" in Portuguese?) Unlike my friend Randy, whose phone chimes "hunka hunka burning love" when his wife calls, I have never been a huge Elvis fan, and I'm surprised by the lack of opulence at his house. Oh, Graceland has plenty of grand features, but I walk away from our visit thinking this shrine to the King of Rock and Roll is as kitschy as it is luxurious, a marriage of the Elvis of Tupelo, Mississippi, and the one of Las Vegas.

It is mid-morning now and we get into our Honda *Odyssey*, christened "Homer" for our voyage, and head south to Oxford to pay homage to William Faulkner. I have made this pilgrimage once before, and I am eager for Susie and Elise to see Rowan Oak, the home of my literary hero. We are the only visitors this early afternoon, and I enjoy talking to the curator, even though he bristles a bit when he learns we are from Charlottesville. Apparently, like many Mississippians, he has not forgiven their native son for bequeathing his papers to the University of Virginia instead of Ole Miss. My favorite room in Rowan Oak is Faulkner's study where he scribbled on the walls the outline for *A Fable*, his 1954 Pulitzer Prize winning novel. Seeing the study this day transports me back to my undergraduate days where for a brief time in the bowels of UVA's Alderman Library one could gaze upon a facsimile of this study, replete with the author's tweed jacket, Underwood typewriter, pipe, and cannonball ashtray.

Our genuflecting done, we climb back into Homer and follow the flat alluvial highways of the Delta to Clarksdale for a two-night stay at the Shack Up Inn. ("Bring your wife, bring your girlfriend; hell, bring 'em both.") Comprised of restored sharecropper shacks surrounding a former cotton gin, the Shack Up Inn attracts blues lovers from around the globe, including we learn, Eric Clapton, Robert Plant, and Elvis Costello. The Shack Up Inn justifiably proclaims, "The Ritz we ain't," a sentiment we endorse when we check into the "Legends Shack" where we discover in the fiberglass shower a vise grip, necessary to turn on and control the flow of the lukewarm water. We walk around the grounds a bit before driving the three miles into town for dinner and music at the Ground Zero Blues Club. When we return to the Legends Shack later that night, we welcome the sight of Moon Pies placed on our pillows.

* * *

Our family's "Blues, Bluegrass, and Barbecue" tour begins in Charlottesville on Independence Day. Elise has graduated from high school the month before and will soon begin her own life of independence in college, albeit just three miles from home at the University of Virginia. We conceive this road trip in the knowledge that it could possibly be our last extended family vacation. Who knows what summer breaks from college might bring not to mention the shrouded years that lurk beyond graduation? Thus, we create an itinerary combining elements of our favorite pastimes: eating, listening to music, and exploring southern history (at least for me).

This first day we leave Charlottesville mid-morning for a Holiday Inn in Bristol, Virginia, "The Birthplace of Country Music." We check into the motel and then follow winding secondary roads to Hiltons, Virginia, and The Carter Family Fold, a concert and performance venue dedicated to old time country and bluegrass music. This site also honors the memory of the first family of country music: A.P., Sara, and Maybelle Carter. Johnny Cash, husband of Maybelle's daughter June, performed at the Fold a number of times (including his last ever concert), and it is with great satisfaction that I take a photo of Elise sitting in the rocking chair of the Man in Black. We enjoy a barbecue dinner on the grounds and take seats in the pavilion bleachers in anticipation of the evening's entertainment, Kody Norris and the Watauga Mountain Boys. All hell breaks loose when the moon-faced, teenage Kody Norris kicks off the first song on his six-string Martin guitar. Members of the previously sedate audience rush to the concrete dance floor and commence clogging, the scene resembling a kind of hillbilly mosh pit. Kody and his boys work up a powerful sweat that evening, as do many of the dancers, but as twilight descends, the music stops, the bass player straps his instrument to the roof of a blue Cadillac DeVille, and the five musicians speed off into the night. We wind our way back to Bristol, our path lit in part by exploding fireworks celebrating our country's founding.

The next afternoon finds us in Nashville after a four-and-a-half hour drive on Interstate 40, Tennessee's version of the Autobahn. Poor Homer could not keep up with the passenger cars and tractor trailers blurring the landscape of the Volunteer State. After checking in at the Doubletree Hotel, we visit the Country Music Hall of Fame, then featuring the exhibit "Family Tradition: The Williams Family Legacy." I admire the music of Hank Williams, whose meteoric crash and burn life inhabits the cosmos of doomed American legends like Paul Bunyan or John Henry. And there's no question the Hillbilly Shakespeare could pen a song to truly break your cheatin' heart. Back in my wannabe guitar player days, Hank's plaintive "Lost Highway" was a mainstay of my six-song repertoire. Each square foot of the massive museum is crammed with artifacts and photographs; touring it is both exhilarating and numbing, and I conclude that this edifice is perhaps best enjoyed with repeated small bites rather than the Golden Corral all you can eat buffet approach we employ.

We return to The Doubletree to digest before heading out to the Bluebird Cafe, a low-slung building in a nondescript strip mall. We arrive early, procure good seats, and order dinner in advance of the 6:30 entertainment. The opening act is JR and the Roadkill Choir and by the reception they receive, we understand that this band is a Music City favorite. JR is all about the entertainment, and for the next hour and a half, he regales the appreciative crowd with some of his classic tunes, like "No Man Was Ever Shot Washing the Dirty Dishes," "I'm Not Drunk Enough to Dance," "You're Too Ugly To Be Cheatin' on Me," and, my favorite, "That's Why Sometimes Daddy's [sic] Need to Drink." You bet I bought the CD after his set.

At 8:00, the first of nine singer-songwriters take the stage; each is afforded a few minutes to showcase his or her tunes and I remember thinking, "How does anyone make it in this business?" Each of the performers is incredibly talented and non-derivative, as far as I can tell, yet I never hear of any of them after that evening. Wait, that's not entirely true. Our favorite of the group is Chris Pickering, a young Australian. We like his soulful songs, his facile guitar playing, and Susie and Elise find him "adorable." A year or two after our road trip, Chris Pickering performs in Charlottesville at The Garage, a tiny art and music space managed by Christ Episcopal Church. At this venue, performers stand in the doorway of the former one-car garage and play to an audience sitting on the hill of a park across an active one way street. Elise is at UVA now and she and I are in the audience for Pickering's show at The Garage. In fact, we *are* the audience, save for the Christ Church volunteer manning the event. After a couple of songs, we tell Chris that we had seen him at The Bluebird, and for the rest of the evening he entertains our requests and tries out some new numbers for our reaction. To his credit, his enthusiasm and musicianship never lags, and it was a special night for Elise and me, if not for him.

* * *

In our lives, we are used to things falling short of expectations, including ourselves of course. So I am skeptical the next morning when at checkout the Doubletree concierge tells us we must visit Loveless Motel and Cafe, home of "the world's best biscuits." After all, he reasons, it is on our way to Memphis, our next destination. Now rightly or wrongly, I do consider myself a bit of a biscuit connoisseur, having grown up in a home where my mother made flaky, from scratch biscuits almost every day. But I have to say the offerings at the Loveless do not disappoint, and after a breakfast of eggs, bacon, and biscuits, we purchase a healthy portion of "the world's best" to help fuel our three-hour drive along truck-infested I-40.

Our first stop is Beale Street, an amalgamation of bars and tourist shops along with a fair number of sidewalk blues buskers. We grab a mid-afternoon barbecue lunch (it was a pork-infused day) before boarding a small bus for the Memphis Mojo Tour. During the next ninety minutes, we make stops at Sun Studio, the Stax Museum, and Soulsville, and along the way our guide points out locales associated with Elvis, B.B. King. Johnny Cash, and others. To supplement this information, our guide, accompanying himself on guitar, performs a number of songs from rockabilly to country to blues to soul. I am impressed. At Sun Studio, "The Birthplace of Rock and Roll," 18-year-old Elise picks up a brochure with the following text:

WHEN THE 18-YEAR-OLD ELVIS WALKED IN TO THE
LEGENDARY SUN STUDIO FOR THE FIRST TIME,
HE WAS ASKED WHO HE SOUNDED LIKE.
AND HE SAID ...

"I DON'T SOUND LIKE NOBODY"

AND HE SANG "THAT'S ALL RIGHT"
LIKE NOBODY EVER HAD ...
WITH THE HONESTY & SOUL OF THE BLUES
AND THE UNLEASHED WILDNESS OF AN ALL NIGHT PARTY!

There you have it.

⁕ ⁕ ⁕

We begin our second day in Clarksdale touring the Delta Blues Museum which houses the shack that was Muddy Waters's boyhood home on Stovall Plantation, a few miles outside of town. To say the structure is a humble one is a huge understatement, and it just goes to show that genius can spring forth from anywhere. We eat lunch at Abe's Bar-B-Q featuring his famous "Come Back Sauce." In addition to the pit-cooked pulled pork, we sample tamales, to me a curious staple of the Delta. We drive over to Kim's Pork Rinds and Cracklins factory and buy a variety of artery-choking wares from the adjacent outlet store. Today, you can order Kim Wong's pork rinds and chicken cracklins direct from the factory and, of course, from Amazon. Finally, we drive by the "colored" hospital where Bessie Smith, the Empress of the Blues, died September 26, 1937 as a result of an automobile accident on Highway 61. It's been another full day as we head back to the Shack Up Inn for our evening Moon Pie.

We are again in Nashville the next afternoon where we resist the temptation to buy cowboy hats in the shops along Broadway before checking in at our old friend The Doubletree. We have tickets that night for the weekly Thursday bluegrass show at the Ryman Auditorium, "The Mother Church of Country Music." It indeed feels like a sacred place; the soft light filtering through the windows illuminates ancient dust motes. We sit in the massive pews and prepare to receive the good news, being proclaimed this evening by Rhonda Vincent and the Rage, the most "awarded" band in bluegrass history. It's a great show and about halfway through, Rhonda Vincent calls to the stage Gaven Largent, a thirteen-year-old dobro playing prodigy from Winchester, Virginia. He is an incredibly gifted instrumentalist who now, ten years later, is a Grammy-nominated member of the bluegrass band Dailey & Vincent, fronted by Jamie Dailey and Darrin Vincent, brother of Rhonda.

The next day, July 10, we hit the road for Charlottesville via a circuitous route that allows for a stopover in Loretto, Kentucky, home of Maker's Mark Distillery, creators of my bourbon of choice. The distillery is an idyllic, sylvan setting and we take the official tour of the grounds and operations. I sign up to become a Maker's Mark "Ambassador," an initiative that results in another road trip eight years later when "my" barrel of whisky matures. Before we leave Loretto, I purchase an unsealed bottle of my favorite hootch and Elise dips it in the brand's signature red wax. It's a proud parental moment, I can tell you that.

Our drive home that afternoon and evening carries us through the mountains of West Virginia. ("Take me home, country roads …") It has been a memorable week full of good food and good music and, more importantly, good times as a family. In the weeks ahead, Elise will leave for college, Susie will become a vegetarian, and I will take full advantage of my Ambassador status. And, oh yeah: B.B. King will keep playing the blues.

Proal Heartwell, 65, lives in Charlottesville, Virginia. He is the co-founder of Village School, where he teaches English. He is also the author of a literary memoir and two novels.

ONE FOR THE ROAD
SPOTIFY PLAYLIST

1. One Fine Day (Carole King)
2. Walk Like a Man (The Four Seasons)
3. Up on the Roof (The Drifters)
4. A Whiter Shade of Pale (Procol Harum)
5. Locomotive Breath (Jethro Tull)
6. Free Bird (Lynyrd Skynyrd)
7. Wooly Bully (Sam the Sham and the Pharaohs)
8. They Drive Around (Bahlmann Abbot)
9. Tie a Yellow Ribbon Round the Ole Oak Tree (Tony Orlando and Dawn)
10. I'm Your Hoochie Coochie Man (Muddy Waters)
11. Spanish Pipedream (John Prine)
12. Route 66 (Chuck Berry)
13. Pompeii (Bastille)
14. Pipeline (The Ventures)
15. Don't Go Breaking My Heart (Elton John & Kiki Dee)
16. Hitch Hike (Rolling Stones)
17. Six Days on the Road (George Thorogood & the Destroyers)
18. If Tomorrow Never Comes (Todd Snider)
19. Cape Cod Kwassa Kwassa (Vampire Weekend)

20. Crazy Mary—Live (Pearl Jam)
21. Here I Go Again (Whitesnake)
22. Carolina in My Mind (James Taylor)
23. Mrs. Robinson—From "The Graduate" (Simon & Garfunkel)
24. Most of All (B.J. Thomas)
25. Early Mornin' Rain (Peter, Paul and Mary)
26. Sports Men (Haruomi Hosono)
27. Upon Viewing Oregon's Landscape with the Flood of Detritus (Titus Andronicus)
28. Clarksdale (Daddy Rich)
29. Crystal Ball Eyes (Super Chikan)
30. Man In Black (Johnny Cash)
31. Lost Highway (Hank Williams)
32. Ruby, Ruby (Chris Pickering)
33. That's All Right (Elvis Presley)
34. All American Bluegrass Girl (Rhonda Vincent & the Rage)
35. See That My Grave Is Kept Clean (B. B. King)

https://open.spotify.com/playlist/002fnF2KORKWTy2LDDhcHB?si=eJRL9z5mSLydSW7MYLqy3g